RSA
TYPEWRITING SKILLS
BOOK TWO

Written for the RSA Examinations Board by
Margaret Rees–Boughton

HEINEMANN
EDUCATIONAL

in association with the RSA Examinations Board

Heinemann Educational,
a division of Heinemann Educational Books Ltd
Halley Court, Jordan Hill, Oxford OX2 8EJ

OXFORD LONDON EDINBURGH
MELBOURNE SYDNEY AUCKLAND
IBADAN NAIROBI GABORONE HARARE
KINGSTON PORTSMOUTH NH (USA)
SINGAPORE MADRID BOLOGNA ATHENS

First published 1987

Reprinted 1987, 1988

Reprinted with amendments 1990

British Library Cataloguing in Publication Data
Rees – Boughton, Margaret
RSA typewriting skills. – 2nd ed.
Bk. 2.
1. Typing
I. Title II. Royal Society of Arts
652.3
ISBN 0 435 45192 8

Design and typesetting by The Pen and Ink Book Company Ltd, London

Foreword

Publication of this book was timed to coincide with the introduction of Stage II of the RSA's new Typewriting Skills examinations, following the warm welcome given to Book One, which related to Stage I. It is designed to help those who have mastered the basic competences and are now aiming to develop the more complex skills involved in the work of the experienced typist.

The Typewriting Skills examination syllabuses set out very precisely what is required of candidates and the criteria by which their work will be assessed. The syllabuses have been developed in such a way as to emphasise the knowledge and skills that are *relevant* and transferable—that will enable the typist to cope competently with any typewriting task in any context, and to comply with the very varied requirements and 'house styles' that may be encountered in the course of employment.

This book guides students authoritatively through each part of the Stage II examination and provides examples and practice material to develop students' competence and confidence in applying their knowledge and skills to the various kinds of realistic task that they will encounter in the examinations—as well as in employment.

As with Book One in this series, the text has been prepared by Margaret Rees-Boughton, Consultant to the RSA in Office Subjects, to whom the RSA here records its thanks.

Martin Cross
Chief Executive
RSA Examinations Board

Note to the 1990 reprint

A number of minor textual amendments have been made to the syllabus and to other parts of this book. These are primarily for clarification and do not significantly alter the substance.

Contents

Section Four   *The Part 2 Exam*

Section Five   Exam Practice

Note: Items B1 – B12 and C1–C14 refer to sections B and C in Parts 1 and 2 of the RSA Typewriting Skills Stage II syllabus (see pages 4–12).

Section One

Introduction

1 *Preparing for RSA Typewriting Skills Stage II*

This book is intended to help candidates prepare for RSA Stage II examinations in Typewriting Skills.

It is explicitly directed at candidates, whether attending full- or part-time courses or studying on their own.

The full syllabus for the examination is included on pages 4–12 so that typists preparing for the award can check:

- what they need to be able to do;
- the type of documents to be used;
- how quickly the work must be completed;
- the degree of accuracy that is essential;
- what will be regarded as faults in presentation.

All of this information is an essential part of training because it provides goals at which to aim.

CHECKING YOUR WORK

Checking and correcting your own work is the best protection against penalties for inaccuracy. In the past, students have sometimes felt that only teachers could decide whether work was right or wrong, because only teachers were versed in 'typewriting theory'. Now, candidates themselves can use the marking scheme included in the syllabus (see pages 9–12) to check on their progress.

The marking scheme is divided into three sections:

- **Rate of Production:** all tasks must be completed (there is a very limited allowance for omissions).
- **Accuracy:** any word that is not 100 per cent accurate is counted as an Accuracy fault. There are **NO** mark allocations and **NO** scales of deductions for errors which may (or may not) be the result of different weaknesses, e.g. spelling, mis-keying.

   Accuracy faults are therefore easy to find and can be simply counted. The number of Accuracy faults allowed in the exam is set out in paragraph 6 of the syllabus (see page 12).
- **Presentation:** the syllabus sets out a list of 'rules' for the presentation of work. These are reduced to essentials and leave most matters of display to be decided by the typist, as in real-life office work.

   The marking scheme (syllabus items C1 to C14) lists occasions when penalties will be incurred, and once again there is no scale of marks to be deducted for different classes of fault.

EXAMINATIONS BOARD

TYPEWRITING SKILLS STAGE II – Summer Series 1989 – 288

Centre Number	YOUR NAMES

THIS FORM—FOR USE IN WORKING TASK 6—MUST BE INSERTED INSIDE THE COVER OF YOUR ANSWER BOOK AT THE CONCLUSION OF THE EXAMINATION. IF BOTH SIDES OF THIS FORM ARE USED ONE ATTEMPT MUST BE CANCELLED.

ORDER FORM

CUSTOMER'S NAME AND ADDRESS	TELEPHONE NO Daytime No only	
	DATE	
	AGENT'S REFERENCE	OPC 666
TOUR NO:	NO OF CLIENTS	

MR/MRS MISS/MSTR	INIT	SURNAME	ROOM TYPE	TOUR PRICE	SUPPLEMENTS ie private facilities etc	
				£		£
				£		£
				£		£
				£		£
				£		£

Balcony   YES/NO*

*Delete as necessary

SUB TOTAL	£	TOTAL £
SUPPLEMENTS	£	
TOTAL TOUR PRICE	£	

DEPOSIT PAID	£
INSURANCE PAID	£
TOTAL PAID	£
BALANCE	£

If you wish to pay by Barclaycard
or Access please tick the appropriate box

VISA [   ]   ACCESS [   ]

[   ]

RSA Typewriting Skills Book Two   Heinemann Educational
© Special copyright conditions apply (see front of stationery pad)

THE SYLLABUS

Chapter 4 contains the Stage II syllabus on which exams will be set from Autumn 1989. The syllabus includes aims, objectives, marking scheme and pass criteria.

The Stage II exam, as described in the syllabus, is set in two parts.

THE EXAM

Some of the assessment objectives of the syllabus apply to both parts of the exam. Section Two of the book covers these general points.

Parts 1 and 2

Section Three covers Part 1 of the exam, and is followed by a section on Part 2.

PRACTICE MATERIAL

Included in Sections Two to Four are exercises for practising the particular syllabus objectives.

Timed exam practice

Timed exam practice material includes typical exam tasks with target times. In the stationery section at the back of the book is a personal progress record for you to fill in, so that you can monitor your progress as you prepare for the exam.

PAST EXAM PAPERS

Two complete Stage II exam papers are included in Section Five as further material for timed exam practice.

STATIONERY

Letterheads, memos and forms needed for completing some of the tasks are included in the stationery section at the back of the book.

WHAT YOU NEED TO KNOW

The book assumes that you have progressed beyond the beginner stage in typewriting. Before starting the learning material here you need to know exactly how your typewriter works.

You should also be familiar with routine documents, that is, letters and memos.

Fictitious details

Names of products, companies or individuals and addresses, etc., used in exam drafts are fictitious. Be careful that you copy these details accurately (see also syllabus item B8 on page 47).

TASK 6

Please complete the Order Form using today's date.

CUSTOMER   Mr Paul Adams. He lives at Stonebank, West Street, WELLINGTON, Telford   TF2 9JS.

The tour no is 975 DFJ and there will be 4 clients. Please type the clients' details on the form.

	Room type	tour price
Paul Adams	shared double	£389
Donna Adams	"	£389

Mr + Mrs Adams will require private facilities + their supplements will be £12 each.

Their children (Peter age 8 and Julie age 10) will require single rooms. Their tour price will be £195 ea with single room supplements of £8 ea.

The supplements total   £40
Tour price sub-total -   £1168
Total tour price   -   £1208

Mr Adams has paid a deposit of £300. No insurance has been paid so the total paid will be £300. The balance will be £908. He will pay the final a/c by ACCESS but as yet we don't have his Access no. Put a 'tick' in the Access Box.

A balcony is not required.   Leave the telephone number blank.

RSA TYPEWRITING SKILLS STAGE I

Beginner typists are usually expected to:

- transfer the writer's words on to appropriate stationery;
- spell in full words shortened in handwritten drafts;
- correct obvious errors in typewritten drafts;
- find facts from one part of a document for inclusion on another occasion within the same task.

THE NEXT STEP

The range and scope of tasks will be extended for the typist who has progressed beyond the beginner stage, and may include:

- routine correspondence and general documentation with more complicated editing and alterations than would be given to the beginner;
- requests to re-arrange or modify material on behalf of the writer.

The more experienced typist can also be relied upon to:
- carry out routine tasks without supervision;
- maintain high standards of work despite the distractions that occur in any office;
- work at an increased rate of production.

RSA TYPEWRITING SKILLS STAGE II

The RSA Stage II exam in Typewriting Skills is set in two parts.

Part 1

This tests your ability to:

a) **Produce correspondence and general documentation** from edited/altered drafts;
b) **Cope with distraction.** Only two of the three tasks you are expected to do in Part I will be given to you at the beginning of the exam. Task 3 will be placed on your desk by the invigilator between 15 and 30 minutes after the starting time.

Part 2

This tests your ability to:

a) **Re-arrange text and modify** layouts;
b) **Allocate space** to produce, for example, a form, a table and a notice or draft advertisement.

TASK 5

Retain abbreviations

LAKE DISTRICT TOURS

Hotel and Tour	Details		Price[2]
	No of Nights[1]	Supplements	
		Per Person	Per Person
Hotel Plaza HP291 Keswick	14	Single room £14 Private facilities £10	£389
Belvue Hotel BH364 Kendal	15	Private facilities £12	£375
Cumbria Court CC401 Kirby	14	Single room £8 Private facilities £10	£359

Typist – make style of these blocks as first block

1 Prices available for 7 and 21 nights ~~only~~ if required.

✓ 2 Prices ~~listed~~ ~~shown~~ are for holidays taken April – May and September – November Inclusive.

Typist – please re-arrange Hotels in alphabetical order.

The following syllabus will apply with effect from the 1989 Autumn series of examinations.

1 AIMS

This scheme defines typewriting competence as a totality of speed, accuracy and presentation skills. Candidates will therefore be assessed in each of these three elements and for award of a certificate must meet the criteria specified for all three of them.

The overall aim of the scheme is to test the candidate's ability to meet the typewriting requirements of the discerning employer.

2 TARGET POPULATION

The person with sufficient skill, sound command of English, basic numeracy and knowledge of business practice, to carry out routine typewriting work without supervision.

The Stage II scheme tests knowledge and skill at a level suitable for employment as a reliable general typist.

3 ASSESSMENT OBJECTIVES

The Objectives listed below will be tested in an examination divided into two parts:

Part 1 tests ability to type general business correspondence and documents composed largely of continuous text.

Part 2 tests ability to present data and text in required formats, e.g. tables, forms, notices.

3.1 Assessment Objectives for Part 1

Section A – Rate of production

A Candidates must use their machines to work at a rate of production* adequate to complete three tasks within 1¼ hours.

Working from handwritten and typewritten drafts, within the three tasks they must produce:

A1 Letter
A2 Memorandum
A3 Two carbon copies of one document
A4 Labels
A5 Article, report, etc., in continuous text

*The production rate at this level takes into account time for: machine manipulation, organisation of time and materials, scanning, reading, interpreting (including use of context to identify words as necessary), use of styles and conventions, checking and correcting, for the purpose of processing drafts in any context. The production rate in Part 1 also takes into account the need to cope with distraction (see paragraph 4.1 below).

Section B – Accuracy of content

B Candidates must use their machines to produce work which, after application of appropriate correction techniques/materials, is accurate in content, including compliance with explicit and implicit instructions (which may be single or composite) about content.

They must:

B1 INSERT date on letters, memos and forms as appropriate, including postdating
B2 LOCATE information in any task for incorporation in another task, as directed

at 4pm for dinner. After your meal we have arranged a display of Irish Dancing.

[The following day we will travel via Galway, the west coast harbour town, which looks out to the Isle of Aran. From here we ~~will~~ travel east to Blarney Castle where you can kiss the Blarney Stone. Finally we will be travelling to Cork for our last overnight stay before we start our journey home.

Book early and enjoy this "Romantic Ireland Luxury Coach Tour".

Use any method to emphasise the names of the hotels every time they occur.

B3 INCORPORATE amendments to text:

a) deletions with replacement
b) deletions without replacement
c) correction signs:

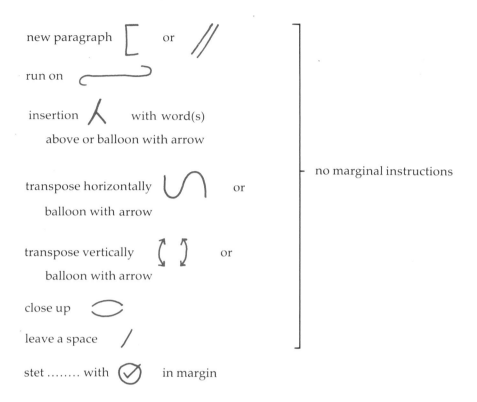

new paragraph [or //

run on

insertion ∧ with word(s)
above or balloon with arrow

transpose horizontally or
balloon with arrow

transpose vertically or
balloon with arrow

close up

leave a space

} no marginal instructions

stet .... with ⊘ in margin

B4 a) SPELL the following words accurately from the abbreviations as shown:

accom	accommodation	incon	inconvenient/ence
a/c(s)	account(s)	info	information
ack	acknowledge	mfr(s)	manufacturer(s)
advert(s)	advertisement(s)	misc	miscellaneous
altho'	although	necy	necessary
appt(s)	appointment(s)	opp(s)	opportunity/ies
approx	approximate/ly	org	organisation
asap	as soon as possible	p/t	part time
bel	believe	poss	possible
bus	business	rec(s)	receipt(s)
cat(s)	catalogue(s)	rec	receive
cttee(s)	committee(s)	recd	received
co(s)	company/ies	recom	recommend
def	definite/ly	ref(s)	reference(s)
dev	develop	refd	referred
ex	exercise	resp	responsible
exp(s)	expense(s)	sec(s)	secretary/ies
exp	experience	sep	separate
f/t	full time	sig(s)	signature(s)
gov(s)	government(s)	suff	sufficient
gntee(s)	guarantee(s)	temp	temporary
hrs	hours	thro'	through
immed	immediate/ly		

TASK 4

Change "coach" to "luxury coach" throughout

PRAXI TOURS LUXURY COACH HOLIDAYS

Romantic Ireland Luxury Coach Tour

Typist - leave a space of at least 50 mm (2") here for an illustration. Also inset the first para 10 spaces.

→ inset 10 spaces

Spend your holiday in romantic Ireland and travel with us by luxury coach from your local departure point to the well-known Bedford Hotel. Here you will be given tea and biscuits before the drive to Holyhead where you will board the afternoon ferry to Dun Laoghaire. You will then be driven by luxury coach to Dublin for your overnight stay at the Bray Boat Hotel.

In the morning we will show you the sights of fair Dublin city. You may like to pay a visit to Trinity College which we believe is the oldest University in Ireland. We will also show you a lovely open public park and the Regency houses of Merrion Square where we understand Oscar Wilde spent his childhood. Lunch will be taken at a well-known local Inn.

The day will end with a glimpse of Dublin Castle and the famous Guinness Brewery. We will return to your hotel (the Park Royal)

sh	shall	wl	will
shd	should	yr(s)	year(s)
wh	which	yr(s)	your(s)
wd	would	dr	dear
w	with		

days of the week (e.g. Thurs, Fri)
months of the year (e.g. Jan, Feb)
words in address (e.g. Cres, Dr)
complimentary closes (e.g. ffly)

b) and RETAIN other commonly used abbreviations such as 'NB', 'etc', 'eg', '&' in company names etc. (handwritten sign '&' in text to be expanded)

B5 INSERT special marks e.g. Confidential, Attention line, as instructed

B6 INDICATE ENCLOSURES as implied in the draft

B7 SELECT and TRANSFER appropriate details to two labels as instructed

B8 COPY unfamiliar and/or foreign words from legible draft

B9 PRESENT IN CORRECTED FORM material containing:

a) typographical errors
b) obvious errors of agreement and punctuation, including apostrophes
c) spelling errors – not confined to the words in Objective B4

These will be indicated in the draft by circling the incorrect word(s) but will not be confined to one specified task in typescript.

B10 ROUTE carbon copies as instructed

Section C – Presentation of work

C Candidates must use their machines to produce work which, after application of appropriate correction techniques/materials, is effectively presented and in line with current styles and conventions – including compliance with explicit and implicit instructions (which may be single or composite) about presentation.
    They must:

C1 SELECT and USE limited supplies of stationery economically and effectively

C2 PRODUCE clean, uncreased work

C3 ENSURE CONSISTENCY throughout a task in the style or form of presentation (at own discretion in the absence of instructions) of the following:

a) abbreviations indicating measurements/weights/times/money
b) words/figures, i.e. using words and/or figures systematically for quantities
c) words/symbols (including dash/hyphen key for 'to'), e.g. % or per cent; May - June or May-June
d) punctuation (open or full style; spacing system)
e) paragraphing including numbered/lettered paragraphs, sub-paragraphs and listed items (indented or blocked; spacing system)
f) alternative spellings
g) fractions
h) line spacing within and between paragraphs, listed items

RSA

EXAMINATIONS BOARD

S288

TYPEWRITING SKILLS
STAGE II (INTERMEDIATE) - PART 2
THURSDAY 8 JUNE 1989

(TIME ALLOWED - ONE AND A QUARTER HOURS)

Notes for candidates

1. Please write or type your name and centre number on each piece of your work.

2. Please assemble your completed work in the order in which it is presented in this paper and cross through any work which you do not wish to be marked.

3. Calculators, English and mother-tongue dictionaries, on-line spellcheckers and centre-prepared or manufacturers' machine manuals may be used in the examination.

4. This paper includes Tasks 4, 5 and 6 which form the whole of Part 2 of the examination.

You must:

1. Complete all three tasks.

2. Use only the stationery provided in your answer book.

3. Insert today's date on forms, unless otherwise instructed.

(Penalties will be incurred if these instructions are not followed.)

TSII-2 (Summer 1989)   © RSA 1989

C4   USE capitals, spaced capitals, initial capitals with underlining and insetting, for emphasis in headings and in text, as shown in draft

C5   USE CONSISTENTLY blocked *or* centred style at own discretion for same type of item throughout a task (e.g. paragraphs in one style and headings in another is not a fault)

C6   USE specified line spacing

C7   ALLOCATE SPACE of specified size which will be expressed in terms of line spaces

C8   USE, in the absence of instructions, regular left-hand and top margins of *at least* 13 mm (½")

C9   LEAVE, in the absence of instructions, a minimum of one clear line space:

  a) before and after headings
  b) **not applicable to Part 1**
  c) between complimentary close and signatory
  d) before and after separate items within a document, e.g. date, reference

C10   USE correcting materials/techniques as necessary to make inconspicuous corrections

C11   INSERT information against pre-printed headings on letters and memos

3.2 Assessment Objectives for Part 2

Section A – Rate of production

A   Candidates must use their machines to work at a rate of production* adequate to complete 3 tasks within 1¼ hours.
    Working from handwritten drafts they must produce:

A6   Pre-printed form completed with given information
A7   Notice or draft advertisement
A8   Table with three columns, one of which will be sub-divided, and multi-line headings

*The production rate at this level takes into account time for: machine manipulation, organisation of time and materials, scanning, reading, interpreting (including use of context to identify words as necessary), use of styles and conventions, checking and correcting, for the purpose of processing drafts in any context. In Part 2 there is greater emphasis on time needed for interpretation of requirements and for formatting documents.

Section B – Accuracy of content

B   Candidates must use their machines to produce work which, after application of appropriate correction techniques/materials, is accurate in content, including compliance with explicit and implicit instructions (which may be single or composite) about content.
    They must:

(N.B. the Part 1 Objectives with the intervening numbers will not be tested in Part 2.)

B3   INCORPORATE amendments to text – as for Part 1 B3

B8   COPY unfamiliar and/or foreign words from legible draft

B11   APPLY AN INSTRUCTION, once given, to all identical instances throughout a task

B12   RULE by hand and/or on the typewriter

This task should be accompanied by a front sheet as in the previous paper.

TASK 3

BEAUTIFUL BRITAIN ← (SPACED CAPS)

(Their) are many places in Britain worth visiting. Ask yr tour operators what they would recom.

Try a holiday in the Lake District.

Stay on the shores of Lake Derwentwater, overlooked by Skiddaw. Keswick is surrounded by spectacular scenery. It has narrow streets, stone houses, bars, shops, Golf and putting. Visit the Century Theatre, Railway Museum, Art Gallery etc.

Tour the lakes travelling through sweeping valleys. Take lunch in a delightful village, bustling with walkers, then proceed to Windermere on the shores of England's Lakeland village. What more could you ask?

Contact your T ———— B ———— now.

Typist - please leave 6 clear lines here for a photograph.

Holiday Highlights

Travel from your local ~~departure~~ pick-ups point

Tour thorugh Englands' finest scenery

All bedrooms have en-suite

Children under 5 travel FREE, over six travel $\frac{1}{2}$ price.

Section C – Presentation of work

C Candidates must use their machines to produce work which, after application of appropriate correction techniques/materials, is effectively presented and in line with current styles and conventions – including compliance with explicit and implicit instructions (which may be single or composite) about presentation.

They must:

(N.B. The Part 1 Objectives with the intervening numbers will not be tested in Part 2.)

C1 SELECT and USE limited supplies of stationery economically and effectively

C2 PRODUCE clean, uncreased work

C3 ENSURE CONSISTENCY throughout a task in a style or form of presentation (at own discretion in the absence of instructions) of the following:

a) abbreviations indicating measurements/weights/times/money
b) words/figures i.e. using words and/or figures systematically for quantities
c) words/symbols (including dash/hyphen key for 'to'), e.g. % or per cent; May - June or May-June
d) punctuation (open or full style; spacing system)
e) paragraphing including numbered/lettered paragraphs, sub-paragraphs, listed items (indented or blocked; spacing system)
f) alternative spellings
g) **not applicable to Part 2**
h) line spacing within and between paragraphs, listed items
i) leader dots
j) material in columns

C4 SELECT and USE CONSISTENTLY available methods of emphasis to give prominence to identified sections of a document, e.g. capital letters, insetting, underlining, varied line-spacing, enumeration, paragraph and heading styles, emboldening.

C5 USE CONSISTENTLY blocked *or* centred style at own discretion for the same type of item throughout a task (e.g. paragraphs in one style with headings in another is not a fault)

C7 ALLOCATE SPACE of specified size (which will be expressed in terms of measurement) e.g. for illustrations

C8 USE, in the absence of instructions, regular left-hand and top margins of at least 13 mm (½″)

C9 LEAVE, in the absence of instructions, a minimum of one clear line space:

a) before and after headings
b) before footnotes
c) **not applicable to Part 2**
d) before and after separate items within a document, e.g. date, reference

C10 USE correcting materials/techniques as necessary to make inconspicuous corrections

C12 From instructions provided, RE-ARRANGE details

C13 From instructions or models provided, MODIFY LAYOUT to conform to a given 'house–style' or to meet specific requirements

C14 INSERT given information on pre-printed forms; MAKE DELETIONS effectively

---

TASK 2

Typist - 2 ccs please, 1 yellow for the File, the other for — David Bosworth
INDICATE ROUTING

(Memo)

From   Tony Greenaway   Ref   TG/TR43
To   Alan Abbot

CONFIDENTIAL

I have recd info with reference to holidays taken in Britain + Europe. The figures below, as you wl see, are very poor and I must ask you to let me have yr comments asap.

Typist - use double line spacing for these items please

a   Holidays in England - ~~up~~ ~~down~~ 30%

b   Holidays in Scotland - up   3 percent

c   "   in Europe - up   70 %

d   Weekend breaks in Britain- up   45 %

(✓)

These figures indicate we shd be looking at how we ~~may~~ can make holidays in Britain more ~~more~~ popular. // I recommend you arrange a meeting w the Tourist board urgently. My contact with them is Ann Leighton, Tour Co-ordinator (UK), Bristol Office.   I would suggest Fri of next week, let my sec have details.

typist - please insert the correct date

1 label please for
David Bosworth
Southern Branch, Praxi Tours Inc
Adam Street, LONDON WC2N 6EZ

4   FORM OF ASSESSMENT

4.1   Candidates will be assessed in two separate 1¼ hour tests set and marked by the RSA. Each part will consist of three practical typewriting tasks. Part 1 will be presented in handwriting and typescript and Part 2 in handwriting.

In Part 1, in order to subject candidates to distraction (see *Production rate in paragraph 3.1 Section A above) Task 3 will be issued by the Invigilator approximately 15–30 minutes after the start of work.

4.2   Nature of tasks: the material given will be:
a) such as is likely to be routinely and ordinarily given to a general typist in the office
b) concerned with topics drawn from the business functions common to the majority of business, commerce and professional offices; e.g. purchasing, personnel, accounts. In Part 1 at least two of the tasks will be within the context of one particular organisation.

4.3   The stationery provided for completion of the tasks will be:

Part 1				Part 2	
A4 letterhead	2	Strip of 3 labels		A4 plain white	4
A4 memo	2	(7.5 cm x 5 cm (3" x 2"))	1	A5 plain white	2
A4 yellow flimsy	4	A5 plain white	2	Printed form	
A4 plain white	2			for completion	2

No additional stationery will be allowed.

4.4   Instructions not under B3 will be given in handwriting and circled to distinguish them from the text.

4.5   Candidates may use calculators, English and mother-tongue dictionaries, on-line spellcheckers, calendars and centre-prepared or manufacturers' machine manuals in the examination. The RSA does not provide these or carbon paper or correcting materials, and candidates are advised to check with their centres well before the examination whether they need to bring any of them.

4.6   Any form of correcting material/correcting mechanism may be used.

5   CRITERIA OF ASSESSMENT

Marking Scheme

Obvious machine faults will not be penalised.

A   *Production Rate* – all tasks, including carbon copies and labels, to be completed (except for 'omissions' at the end of tasks which may be counted within tolerances for Section B, see paragraph 6).
Candidates' work will not be marked under Sections B and C for each Part unless all tasks have been submitted.

B   *Accuracy of content*

An Accuracy fault is ascribed to any word which is not 100% accurate when compared with given test material.

A word is defined as:

a) any normally recognisable word (hyphenated words count as one).
b) any series of characters (including spaces where appropriate) which constitute a recognisable unit, e.g. postcode, initials or groups of initials, courtesy title, line of dots, line of ruling, numbers, simple or compound measurements.
c) including following or associated punctuation and spacing.

up with the Hotel Drei Konige and will (advice) you of our findings just as soon as we ~~rec~~ receive ~~their~~ reply.

(We must admit this is the first time we have (recieved) a complaint of this nature about this hotel but please do not take this as an indication that we doubt what you are saying in any way.

To show good faith we are enclosing ~~cheques~~ vouchers for £150 towards the cost of your next British holiday. This holiday must however be booked within 1 yr from the date of this letter or alternatively you may use the vouchers as payment towards any day excursions taken during the next 2 years. Perhaps we could suggest Blackpool Illuminations, Christmas shopping in London or a day in Llandudno. Do contact us for further details.

Should you decide to take your holiday during the "off-peak" months we will deduct 15% from the cost of the holiday. We will also provide you with 3-star holiday insurance and a taxi to and from your home at the start + finish of your holiday. Finally we apologise for any incon caused and hope this will not deter you from travelling with Praxi Tours Inc again.

Yours scly

Janis M Grainger (Ms)

1 label please
for the addressee

One Accuracy fault only will be ascribed to any one word (e.g. 'acom–odatoin' counts only as one Accuracy fault in spite of several faults in the word) but Presentation faults may be applied in addition (e.g. dates inappropriately aligned against pre-printed heading).

The same fault appearing more than once counts as an Accuracy fault each time.

Copies will be treated in the same way as all other pieces of work and will be marked in the usual way, *except* that faults already penalised on the first copy (original) will not be penalised again on the second copy.

There are three main types of Accuracy fault:

1 *Typing/spelling/punctuation faults*

These are words which:
1.1 contain a character which is incorrect or illegible for any reason
1.2 have omitted or additional characters or spaces within the word (including omissions caused by faulty use of correction materials/ techniques, e.g. hole in paper)
1.3 contain handwritten character(s) – except accents, etc.
1.4 have no space following them;
    have more than two spaces following them, except where appropriate, e.g. in spaced capitals, before postcode, in work with justified margins;
    (symbols and figures (e.g. £10), measurements (e.g. 3' 6"), etc. count as one word (see (b) above) and may include spaces if used systematically – see C3)
1.5 contain overtyping, including overtyping of pre-printed material (per entry regardless of the number of words involved) in letters, memos and forms
    (Satisfactory stretching or squeezing of words causing touching of characters without overlapping will not be penalised)
1.6 do not contain initial capitals in essential instances, e.g. for proper nouns and at the beginning of sentences, or contain grammatically incorrect initial capitals.
    (Failure to insert a capital following a penalty for an omitted full stop will not be penalised.)

2 *Omissions and additions*

An Accuracy fault will be ascribed to:
2.1 each word which is
    – the wrong word (replacing a word)   – omitted (and not replaced)
    – added (not replacing a word)   – not removed as instructed
2.2 penalties for omission of *implied* instructions will be limited to the minimum number of words essential to fulfil the objective
    – for failure to indicate enclosure   – for failure to indicate routing
2.3 each instance of failure to indicate paragraph as per draft

3 *Transpositions and misplacements*

One Accuracy fault will be ascribed to each instance of words
    – not transposed in accordance with an amendment to text under Objective B3
    – inserted in wrong order or place in the absence of an instruction under Objective C12 to re-arrange (see C12 below), eg misplaced within text or as foot or marginal note, regardless of the amount of material involved (in addition to any Accuracy faults which may be incurred under B1 above).

C   *Presentation of work*

One Presentation fault is recorded for each:
C1   task on incorrect stationery

TASK 1

Our ref JMa/AFG

Mrs D Beany
Plovers Barn
YATELEY
Surrey   YA3 7BH

Typist — I realise this will be a bit of a squash so just leave margins of ½". It may help also if you just leave 2 lines for my signature

Dr Mrs Beany

Thank you for yr recent letter. We were very sorry indeed to (here) of the problems you have experienced during your recent trip to Spain & Italy. You will of course appreciate it is not always poss to control events that may occur when you holiday out of Britain. We do altho' try to ensure that every possible [effort & care] are taken by the tour operator to give you value for money. However it has to be said that on the odd occasion things can sometimes go wrong. // Our immed ~~observations~~ ~~investigations~~ do in fact show that your booking was most def without fault. This is confirmed by the tour operator's booking form. A copy of the form is (attached) so you can see for yourself. We are taking this matter

C2 task dirty (e.g. thumb marks, eraser stains, typing on reverse), creased or torn
(N.B. it is not necessary to fold or tear A4 memo paper but if this is done cleanly and effectively no penalty will be incurred.)

C3 inconsistency in items (a) to (j) – ONE penalty only throughout a task for each item:

a) abbreviations indicating measurements/weights/times/money
b) words/figures – words and figures used randomly for quantities
c) words/symbols (including dash/hyphen key for 'to'), word and symbol used, inconsistent spacing
d) punctuation (at least one space required after punctuation mark)
(N.B. If *no* space, Accuracy fault – see B1.4)
e) paragraphing, including numbered/lettered paragraphs, sub-paragraphs and listed items – indented and blocked used randomly; horizontal spacing inconsistent
f) alternative spellings
g) fractions
h) line-spacing within and between sections
i) leader dots
j) material in columns (i.e. blocked/indented/centred). Whole *figures* may be ranged to the left or the right of a column; *words* may be ranged to the left, blocked or centred

C4 *Part 1*

instance of capitals/spaced capitals/initial capitals with underlining, insetting, for emphasis in headings and in text not as shown in the draft.
(Unrequested underlining of headings will not be penalised. Consistent incorrect use of capitals and/or underlining in related headings within a task will incur one penalty only.)

Part 2 – task in which indicated details not emphasised consistently.

C5 a) task in which blocked or centred style (at own discretion) not used consistently for the same type of item throughout a task
(e.g. paragraphs in one style with headings in another style is not a fault).

b) centred style headings and/or material not technically accurate to within 13 mm (½″) horizontally. (N.B. one fault only if all examples are consistent with a major item centred inaccurately.)

C6 instance of failure to vary line spacing within a document as instructed.

C7 allocation of space

a) as specified in line spaces not accurate
b) as specified in measurements not *at least* given size

C8 top margin less than 13 mm (½″)
left margin less than 13 mm (½″) } either or both margins

task with irregular left margin not attributable to machine fault, nor to intentional variance for sub-paragraphs, listed items, etc.

C9 instance of *no* clear line space in the absence of instructions at points (a) – (d) – ONE penalty throughout a task for each item:

a) before and after headings
b) before footnotes
c) for signature on letters
d) before and after separate items within a document

EXAMINATIONS BOARD

TYPEWRITING SKILLS
STAGE II (INTERMEDIATE) - PART 1
THURSDAY 8 JUNE 1989

(TIME ALLOWED - ONE AND A QUARTER HOURS)

Notes for candidates

1.   Please write or type your name and centre number on each piece of
     your work.

2.   Please assemble your completed work in the order in which it is
     presented in this paper and cross through any work which you do not
     wish to be marked.

3.   Calculators, English and mother-tongue dictionaries, on-line
     spellcheckers and centre-prepared or manufacturers' machine manuals may
     be used in the examination.

4.   This paper includes Tasks 1 and 2; Task 3 will be handed to you during the
     course of the examination.

You must:

1.   Complete all three tasks.

2.   Use only the stationery provided in your answer book.

3.   Insert today's date on letters and memos, unless otherwise instructed.

(Penalties will be incurred if these instructions are not followed.)

TSII-1 (Summer 1989)   ©RSA 1989

C10 instance (may be one or more words) of unsightly and conspicuous correction that results in:

a) characters appearing blurred or bold in contrast with uncorrected work

b) smoothness of paper being impaired by raised peaks of correcting fluid (no penalty for unavoidable raised effect of use of fluid or stick-on tapes/strips)

c) substantial mis-alignment of character(s) – i.e. half-line space or more (no penalty for direct typing on carbon copies for correction purposes)

d) hole in paper – unless already penalised under B1.2 as an Accuracy fault.

(White correcting fluid on coloured stationery will not be penalised.)

C11 entry inappropriately inserted against pre-printed headings on letters, memos and forms, regardless of number of words involved (e.g. more than one line space above and below) – **NB**: Part 1 only

C12 each two items not rearranged as instructed (e.g. five faults if ten items) **NB** these penalties apply *only* for Part 2 instructions to re-arrange details

C13 each aspect of modification not carried out as instructed (e.g. layout of headings not changed, items in columns not moved to horizontal layout – two faults).

C14 information inappropriately inserted on pre-printed forms (i.e. more than one line space above or below) **NB**: Part 2 only

6   CERTIFICATION

6.1 Results for each part of the examination will be graded Distinction, Pass or Fail.

6.2 For award of a **Stage II Part 1 Certificate with Distinction** candidates must fulfil

Objective A   by working at a production rate of 600 words per hour in Part 1 (i.e. completing all three tasks);

Objective B   with no more than four Accuracy faults; *and*

Objective C   with no more than four Presentation faults

For award of a **Stage II Part 2 Certificate with Distinction** candidates must fulfil

Objective A   by working at a production rate of 360 words per hour in Part 2 (i.e. completing all three tasks);

Objective B   with no more than three Accuracy faults; *and*

Objective C   with no more than three Presentation faults

6.3 For award of a **Stage II Part 1 Pass Certificate** candidates must fulfil

Objective A   by working at a production rate of 600 words per hour (i.e. completing all three tasks);

Objective B   with no more than eleven Accuracy faults; *and*

Objective C   with no more than eight Presentation faults

For award of a **Stage II Part 2 Pass Certificate** candidates must fulfil

Objective A   by working at a Production Rate of 360 words per hour (i.e. completing all three tasks);

Objective B   with no more than seven Accuracy faults; *and*

Objective C   with no more than five Presentation faults

6.4 The results slips issued to all candidates will indicate the grade awarded in each of the two parts of the examination.

6.5 Candidates who pass both Parts will be awarded a certificate for each Part and qualify for a full Stage II certificate. For a full Stage II certificate with Distinction candidates must achieve a distinction for both Part I and Part 2.

EXAMINATIONS BOARD

TYPEWRITING SKILLS STAGE II — Whitsun Series 1989 – 288

Centre Number	YOUR NAMES

THIS FORM—FOR USE IN WORKING TASK 6—MUST BE INSERTED INSIDE THE COVER OF YOUR ANSWER BOOK AT THE CONCLUSION OF THE EXAMINATION. IF BOTH SIDES OF THIS FORM ARE USED ONE ATTEMPT MUST BE CANCELLED.

EXPENDITURE APPLICATION

Name: Ref No:

Address: Date:

		Unit Price	Total Price
		£	£
Function: Brief Details: Date: Catering: No. attending: Additional requirements: Copy correspondence * delete as appropriate	 Enclosed/not enclosed*		
		Total	£

RSA Typewriting Skills Book Two   Heinemann Educational
© Special copyright conditions apply (see front of stationery pad)

Section Two

The Whole Exam

5	*Rate of Production*

In each part of the exam you will need to complete three tasks in 1¼ hours.

In Part 1 these will be :

a) a letter
b) a memo   } on A4 paper
c) a piece of continuous text (e.g. an article or an extract from a report) on either A4 or A5 plain paper

You will also be required to take two carbon copies; and to address two labels.

In Part 2 the three tasks will be:

a) details to be entered on to a pre-printed form
b) a notice or draft advertisement
c) a ruled table

READING TIME INCLUDED

No special time is allowed for reading through drafts. You must allocate time for this during the exam, just as you take time to set margins, check and correct your work, and for all the other activities that make up typewriting skills.

In Part 2 you will need time for planning, rearranging material and modifying layout. For this reason, the number of words to be typed is considerably less in Part 2 than in Part 1.

IMPROVING YOUR RATE OF PRODUCTION

To improve your production rate drill and practise:

1 keyboarding

a) Use straightforward text to develop keying-speed.
b) Time your typing of unfamiliar and complicated material to develop concentration.
c) Type drills that concentrate on characters you regularly mis-key.

2 correcting techniques

a) Remove and replace words or characters.
b) Remove word(s) that will not be replaced by others (your correction may be more easily seen).
c) Correct carbon copies.

3 setting-up

a) Insert and straighten paper.
b) Set margins.
c) Clear and set tab stops.

Please complete the Application Form to request expenditure in respect of:
Greensomes Golf & Country Club, LEICESTER LE6 4PZ.
Ref No 41093.

On Saturday 24th June we are planning a special function — Praxi (Golf Gala) Day. We estimate that 80 people will attend, and catering arrangements will be as follows:

Hot and cold fork buffet lunch with wine and coffee (unit price £5.25, Total price £420.00)

Afternoon tea (Unit price £1.50, Total price £120.00)

Additional requirements are:
8⁶ V-neck lambswool sweaters @ £15.99 = £95.94
2 silk ties @ £10.50 = £21.00
2 sports bags @ £20.00 = £40.00
2 sets of golf waterproofs @ £55.00 = £110.00

Final total £806.94

Brief details: Request for funds to sponsor the launch of Praxi Sport in the Leicester area.

Copy correspondence will not be enclosed.

4 machine manipulation

a) *Tabulation*: set six tab stops across the page and
i) type columns of words, concentrating on moving quickly across the page;
ii) type columns of figures, concentrating on use of the space bar to align units, tens, hundreds, etc.

b) *Margin release*: set tab stops at left margin and *in* the margin.
Practise using the margin release with the carriage return. Then use the tabulator to stop in the margin, type the paragraph number, and finally press the tabulator to return to the left margin.

c) *Backspace mechanisms, quick paper release, half spacing*, and other functions available to you on your machine.

- YOU MUST FINISH all six tasks to pass the exam. Up to eleven words in Part 1 and up to seven words in Part 2 may be omitted. All omissions will be counted as Accuracy faults.

- NO SPECIAL READING TIME is allocated.

PERSONAL PROGRESS RECORD

You may be able to complete some types of task more quickly than others, so it is important to time yourself over three tasks which make up one part of the exam.

Timed examination practice is provided in Section Three. The Stage II past exam papers in Section Five will give you the chance of further timed practice.

A personal progress record for you to fill in is included in the stationery section at the back of the book. It will give you the opportunity to monitor your progress.

COPY-TYPING SPEED TEST

There is **no speed test** in RSA Typewriting Skill exams. These exams are concerned only with your rate of production of simulated business tasks, using all of the different skills that make up competence in typewriting relevant to office work.

You may enter a **separate** speed test to show how quickly you can key-in punctuated text.

The copy-typing speed test is open to all. You can enter for this test at any time, as it is not conditional upon your entering an exam in Typewriting Skills at any Stage.

A minimum of 15 words per minute (w.p.m.) must be demonstrated in the 10-minute test. Speeds above 15 w.p.m. are credited in units of 5 w.p.m. that is, at 20/25/30 w.p.m. and upwards.

Full details of this separate test are available from the Publications Section, RSA Examinations Board, Westwood Way, Coventry CV4 8HS.

retain abbreviations

Praxi Sport Retail Outlets (~~as at~~ April 1989)

Typist — make the layout for there the same as for the Birmingham section

Branch	No. of staff		Turnover (excl. VAT) for 1988
	Full-time[1]	Part-time[2]	£
Manchester			
Pitzburg Centre	2	5	125,000
Round End	5	4	253,000
The Court	2	2	82,000
Lion Yard	3	3	91,000
Edinburgh			
High Street	4	5	291,000
Green Road	2	2	141,000
Kingsgate	1	3	80,000
Birmingham			
Church ~~Avenue~~ Street	2	2	105,000
The Mews	6	6	130,000
West Parade	3	2	330,000

[1] Employed to work more than 35 hrs per week
[2] Employed to work less than 35 hrs per week

Please re-arrange the 3 sections so they are in alphabetical order ie Birmingham section first

Throughout the exam you must type all words accurately. Every type of word error is treated in the same way.

FAULTS ARE WORDS WITH

incorrect or illegible character(s)

omitted or additional character(s)

handwritten insertion

overtyping

initial capitals not as shown in draft

omitted words

additional words

more than 2 spaces after them (but this
   is not a fault in special places, eg
   between words in spaced capitals)

IN ADDITION, FAULTS ARE COUNTED FOR

words in the wrong place

By usung these grids i should

be fairly eas to visualise thes

layout of each page as you write,

and hopefully most of the urgenh

problems We had in march can be

avoided. Please hesitate to give

me a ring if if anything further

is   not clear.

It is clear not where we must go.

The marking scheme in the syllabus (see pages 9–12) gives a full description of Accuracy faults.

- ■ All WORDS must be ACCURATE.

- ■ EACH wrong WORD will be COUNTED as an Accuracy fault; each word left out or added will be counted.

CHECK YOUR ACCURACY

To be awarded a Pass in Part 1 of the exam you must complete the three tasks with no more than eleven uncorrected errors. To gain Distinction your work should include no more than four Accuracy faults.

   In Part 2, you must not leave more than seven uncorrected errors for the award of a Pass. If your work includes three or less Accuracy faults you may be awarded a Distinction for Accuracy.

   (To be awarded a Pass or Distinction overall, you need to work at the required rate of production so as to complete all six tasks in the paper and maintain the standards of presentation (see page 12) *as well as* accuracy.)

Praxi Sport Ltd
GRAND SPORTSWEAR SALE
to be held on
Friday 2nd June and Saturday 3rd June 1989
at all our Manchester Branches

change "per item" to "each" throughout please

Come in and see what great bargains are on offer.
Sale starts at 7.30 am on Friday (June 2nd)!

Star Bargains - Limited Number Available At Crazy Prices!
V-neck sweaters, all sizes and colours . . . . . . £8.99 per item
Cotton T-shirts for ladies, lemon or pink . . . . . £2.99 per item
Cotton T-shirts for men, white or aqua . . . . . £1.99 per item
Sports socks, various - . . . . £0.30 per pair
Cotton shorts for men, navy only . . . . £2.50 per pair
Swimwear for men and women . . . . £3.50 per item

Typist - leave a space of at least 63 mm (2½") please for an illustration

Other attractions ~~over the 2 days~~ include a golf professional at Round End Branch and a tennis coach at Lion Yard ↑ on (Branch) Friday 2nd June from 5.00 pm to 9.00 pm. They will be
✓ available for FREE ~~advice~~ !

At the Pitzburg Centre delicious cocktails will be served during the early evening, whilst at The Court all customers over the sale period will be entered in a complimentary champagne raffle !

Spend more than ~~£15~~ £20 and you will be entitled to free entry in our fantastic prize draw. You could win 2 tickets to Wimbledon !

All stock reduced by 20 %, so do come along!

Typist - use any method to emphasize the words marked

There are some general requirements for presentation of all your work in both parts of the exam. These are concerned with:

- stationery (see also Section Four);
- clean and uncreased work;
- blocked or centred styles;
- margins
- space between items;
- corrections.

These are discussed in this chapter, that is, syllabus items C1, C2, C5, C8, C9 and C10.

CHECK YOUR PRESENTATION

The full marking scheme for presentation appears on pages 10–12.

You must complete the exam tasks with no more than eight presentation faults in Part 1, and no more than five presentation faults in Part 2.

If you can complete the work with no more than four presentation faults in Part 1, and no more than three presentation faults in Part 2 you will gain a Distinction for Presentation.

(To be awarded a Pass or Distinction overall, you need to work at the required rate of production so as to complete the paper and maintain the standards of accuracy (see page 12) *as well as* presentation.)

C1   STATIONERY

You must use the correct stationery for each task. There will be sufficient paper for you to make two attempts, if necessary, at each task. The exception is the labels required in Part 1. You will receive three of these, but will need to use two in a task.

No extra stationery will be supplied or should be used in the exam.

You will receive a presentation penalty for any task typed on the wrong stationery.

C2   CLEAN AND UNCREASED WORK

The work that you produce in the exam must be clean and uncreased.

All it takes is care

- **Watch your carbon paper:**
  keep the shiny side away from you;
  use the paper release when putting carbon paper into your machine;
  protect carbon copies when correcting;
  handle gently.
- **Keep your hands clean:**
  have paper tissues handy and use them often.
- **Organise your work area:**
  the more you have to search for pens, ruler, dictionary, correcting materials, etc., the greater the risk of dirtying, creasing and having accidents with carbons and fluids.

EXAMINATIONS BOARD

 TYPEWRITING SKILLS
STAGE II (INTERMEDIATE) - PART 2
TUESDAY 2 MAY 1989

(TIME ALLOWED - ONE AND A QUARTER HOURS)

Notes for candidates

1. Please write or type your name and centre number on each piece of
    your work.

2. Please assemble your completed work in the order in which it is
    presented in this paper and cross through any work which you do not
    wish to be marked.

3. Calculators, English and mother-tongue dictionaries, on-line
    spellcheckers and centre-prepared or manufacturers' machine manuals may
    be used in the examination.

4. This paper includes Tasks 4, 5 and 6 which form the whole of Part 2 of
    the examination.

————————————

You must:

1. Complete all three tasks.

2. Use only the stationery provided in your answer book.

3. Insert today's date on forms, unless otherwise instructed.

(Penalties will be incurred if these instructions are not followed.)

TSII-2 (Whitsun 1989 - 288)   © RSA 1989

- **Don't deliberately tear stationery:**
  It is not necessary to tear or fold A4 stationery for short tasks. Many offices use only one size of printed stationery. It is better to shape your work by varying margins and line spacing than to waste time ruling and cutting.

- DON'T RUSH! Go gently. Select stationery carefully. Keep tidy and clean.

- SHAPE YOUR WORK for easy reading.

- SEARCHING for fluid, rubber, pens etc., causes accidents!

Should you be unfortunate enough to spoil the stationery provided for a particular task, it is advisable to re-type the task on whatever paper you still have available. **Remember**, to pass the exam you must complete every task.

C5   BLOCKED OR CENTRED STYLES

The syllabus allows you to use blocked or centred style, whichever you prefer. You will not be required to centre work either horizontally (with equal margins at left and right) or vertically (with equal margins at top and bottom).

You need not type an entire task in the same style (although you may choose to do it in this way if you wish). For example, centred headings may be used with block paragraphs.

What is important is that all instances of the same type of item are presented in the same style, e.g. several sub-headings in a letter or report.

```
Report to General Manager


         SPRING CATALOGUE

Coats

Many new items will be included,   Prices
will range from £20 to £95.

Dresses

No winter items will be included.  All
stock is in full range of sizes 8-22.


            AGENCIES

Overseas

Agents have now been appointed in Italy
and France, and negotiations are in hand
to appoint a Belgian agent in December.

United Kingdom

Southsea and Harrogate offices have been
closed.  New agencies are now operating
in Bradford, Morecambe and Telford.
```

```
30 Pebble Fields
Wolverhampton
WV20 6FD

7 September 1987


Messrs J & M Dudies
29 Havings Row
BIRMINGHAM   B90 2FA


Dear Sirs

Leaseholds

    I am not yet able to complete the
documents for 99 Abulson Street.

Trustees

    All of the nominations have been
confirmed, and deeds are being drawn
up.

      Yours faithfully


      J D Howe
```

Letter to: F Way Esq, The Secretary, Greensomes Golf & Country Club, LEICESTER LE6 4PZ, our ref ND/G389

address a label as well Please

Dr Mr Way

Praxi Sport Ltd will ~~soon~~ ~~shortly~~ be opening a retail outlet in yr area, selling quality sportswear.

At the same time as launching our Praxi sportswear range ~~there~~ locally, we are ~~anxious~~ keen to sponsor a limited number of competitions at selected sports clubs. // Perhaps you wd like to show the notice enclosed (typist insert title P— G— G— D—) to yr cttees. Please inform me asap wether suff members are interested.

May I suggest Sat 24th June?

Please telephone me if you wish to discuss catering etc in more detail.

Yrs sincly

Nicholas Driver
Marketing Director

Using centred style

You may centre on the paper width (that is, at equal distances from left and right edges of the paper); or you may centre over your typing line (that is, at equal distances from your left and right margins). Whichever you choose, the centring needs to be accurate to within 13 mm (½ in.)–see the marking scheme for C5 (page 11).

```
Centring over the typing line



    Dear Sirs

          Statements

    We have been able to arrange for
    your Statements of Account to be
    forwarded to you by the 5th of
    each month.

          Discount

    This will be at the usual rate
    for accounts such as yours.

          Yours faithfully
          D & J BOOTHRID


          Accountant
```

```
Centring over the paper width:



    G M   M O T O R   C O M P A N Y


            Announcement



         Our new address:

         29-47 Highton Ways
              Dimblong
               HULL
              HU45 8TX



         GRAND OPENING:

              Friday
              Next
```

■ CENTRING TAKES TIME. Remember, you must complete all of the tasks in order to pass the examination.

C8 MARGINS

In the absence of instructions to leave specific margins in the exam, a general rule that you could follow is:

- on plain A4 leave 25 mm (1 in.) margins all round.
- on plain A5 leave 13 mm (½in.) margins all round.
- on printed paper line up left margins with letter and memo headings.

When typing a short document 'all round' means top and both sides of the paper.

RSA

EXAMINATIONS BOARD

W286

TYPEWRITING SKILLS
STAGE II (INTERMEDIATE) - PART 1
TUESDAY 2 MAY 1989

TASK 3

When typing long documents that are likely to extend to more than one page, 'all round' includes the bottom margin as well. Make a pencil mark in the margin approximately 51 mm (2 in.) from the bottom of the page as advance warning that you are nearing the end of the page – it will remind you not to type beyond 25 mm (1 in.) from the bottom edge.

Use your judgement

As you have moved from the beginner stage and gained more experience, you have developed your skill and judgement in placing material on your stationery so as to give a 'balanced' appearance, that is, a balance between space and text.

```
SUMMER TIMETABLE

New schedules apply from 1 May each
year.  Send for your copy of this year's
table from:

6 Charing Cross Vale, LONDON WC9 42B.

Send a stamped, addressed envelope not
less than 200 mm x 250 mm.
```

```
SUMMER TIMETABLE

New schedules apply from
1 May each year.  Send for
your copy of this year's
table from:

6 Charing Cross Vale
LONDON WC9 42B.

Send a stamped, addressed
envelope not less than
200 mm x 250 mm.
```

Making decisions

In deciding margin widths, you need to take account of:

- **the amount and type of text in the task,** e.g. insets take up more room than continuous text.
- **the size and type of stationery to be used,** e.g. short tasks on A4 need wide margins (and perhaps double-line spacing).
- **the purpose of the document,** e.g. the use of narrow margins to fit work on small paper is more suitable for an internal memo than for a letter to a customer.
- **any special requirements indicated for use of the document,** e.g. 'for insertion in a top-bound file' makes a top margin of 13 mm (½ in.) quite unsuitable.

PRAXI GALA GOLF DAY ← (spaced caps)

SPONSORED BY PRAXI SPORT LTD

(Type this para in double line spacing)

(typist leave 4 clear line spaces here)

Praxi Sport Ltd will be introducing high quality sportswear into this area shortly. We would be delighted to have the opportunity of sponsoring a competition at your Club to promote the superb range of products we offer.

The format we suggest is a 27-hole strokeplay competition with 18 holes being played in the morning and 9 holes in the afternoon. Men and women golfers of all levels are welcome but must hold a current handicap certificate. Numbers have to be ~~restricted~~ limited to 60. Starting times need to commence at 0800 hours Groups of 4 people will play together, starting from the 1st tee at intervals of 8 minutes. A draw will take place 1 week before the competition to decide on the starting time for each player. As there are usually fewer lady golfers than men, we plan to arrange for a group to consist of 3 men and 1 lady in as many instances as possible. //
Praxi Sport Ltd is happy to (to) provide a substantial hot and cold (bufet) lunch with wine and coffee for the players and Committee Members of the Club. We intend, ~~naturally~~ of course, to provide the prizes from our most attractive yet highly practical range of sportswear for men and women. We can also carry out our unique personalizing service on these prizes for the lucky winners!

The main competition will be over the full 27 holes. Prizes will be awarded to both men and women, based on the top 3 net scores for each. Additional prizes will also be presented for the best male and (femail) net scores for the morning and afternoon rounds. A draw is to be held with more (fabulus) prizes to be won! Players' names will automatically be entered in this draw as they commence play.

Tea at around 1700 hours will be followed at 5.45 pm with the presentation of prizes by the Managing Director of Praxi Sport, Derek Wood.

We hope you agree this great competition will be attractive to your members. Please let us know if you have any queries.

                                                    GNTEE
WE AT PRAXI SPORT LOOK FORWARD TO YOUR SUPPORT AND TO PROVIDE EVERY ASSISTANCE IN MAKING THIS EVENT A SUCCESS.

(immed)

- LEFT or TOP margins of LESS THAN 13mm (½ in.) will be counted as Presentation faults in the exam.

- RIGHT and BOTTOM margins are not penalised, but inconsistent line spacing is: if you type to the bottom of the page, the paper may slip and your lines will slope!

- DON'T FORGET to remove your 'reminder' mark warning you not to type too low on the paper.

PRACTICE MATERIAL
Decide the margins that you need before typing the following:

Task 1

Type in double-line spacing. Select size of paper & margins to give your work a balanced appearance.

MARKETING POLICY

Many firms still rely on annual sales to reduce unsold stocks. This traditional method of emptying shelves to make room for new stock is particularly favoured by the clothing industry. Fashions change quickly and last season's goods hold little attraction for some customers. // Retailers have to judge at the beginning of the season how many items, and in what sizes and colours, are likely to be sold. The accuracy of their judgement can sometimes be measured by the end of season sales. // In the food trade, however, it is not possible to buy perishable goods for more than a few days in advance. Most goods are stamped with a date by which they should be sold if they are to reach the customer in prime condition.

This "short season" means the shop workers have to be fully trained and very conscientious in operating the firm's stock control system.

2 ccs please on yellow flimsy, 1 for file and 1 for John Reed who will be the Manager at Leicester Branch. Can you address a label to: Mr J Reed, 81 Bushfield, LEICESTER LE4 4JJ.

memo from Nicholas Driver to Gary Hudson
ref ND-PSL89   URGENT

Praxi Sport Launch, Leicester Area

We are still behind schedule with the preparation of the shop in Church Square. ~~However,~~ I wl be meeting the shop fitters ~~builders~~ on Mon of next week (typist insert date) and hope to resolve ~~solve~~ the problems.

I have circulated several sports clubs:

1 Golf
We have written Today to the 3 clubs in the area ~~with provisional dates~~ and have asked for replies as promptly as poss.

2 Tennis
Tennis is popular this ~~year summer~~. All 6 clubs approached wish to enter the 2-day tournament suggested.

3 Swimming
Of the 5 clubs contacted, two have expressed interest in a gala day.

C9 SPACE BETWEEN ITEMS

RSA syllabuses in Typewriting Skills do not specify any particular style for setting out documents. This is because so many styles are acceptable in the real business world. Executives may have their own preferences while some offices may have 'house rules' on layout. Wherever you work you will need to be flexible so that you can adapt easily to different business requirements.

The basic rule for line spacing is:

> unless a special instruction is given, you must always leave **at least one** clear line space to separate different items within a document.

Space between paragraphs

Paragraphs must be separated from each other, and from other items (e.g. headings) above and below them.

When the text is in double-line spacing, it is common practice to leave two clear lines between paragraphs. Another way to separate paragraphs in double-line spacing is to make sure that a very short line occurs before each new paragraph. This may mean deliberately taking the last word of the paragraph to a new line:

```
Your new passport is enclosed together

with your previous passport which has

been cancelled, but which contains an

'indefinite' visa for the Continent.


Entry is a matter for the issuing

country but it is understood that an

'indefinite' visa remains valid even

though the passport may have expired.


However, as entry regulations are

subject to alteration without warning,

you may wish to obtain advice.
```

```
Your new passport is enclosed together

with your previous passport which has

been cancelled, but which contains an

'indefinite' visa for the

Continent.

Entry is a matter for the issuing

country but it is understood that an

'indefinite' visa remains valid even

though the passport may have

expired.

However, as entry regulations are

subject to alteration without warning,

you may wish to obtain advice.
```

EXAMINATIONS BOARD

TYPEWRITING SKILLS
STAGE II (INTERMEDIATE) - PART 1
TUESDAY 2 MAY 1989

(TIME ALLOWED - ONE AND A QUARTER HOURS)

Notes for candidates

1. Please write or type your name and centre number on each piece of
    your work.

2. Please assemble your completed work in the order in which it is
    presented in this paper and cross through any work which you do not
    wish to be marked.

3. Calculators, English and mother-tongue dictionaries, on-line
    spell checkersand centre-prepared or manufacturers' machine manuals may
    be used in the examination.

4. This paper includes Tasks 1 and 2; Task 3 will be handed to you during the
    course of the examination.

You must:

1. Complete all three tasks.

2. Use only the stationery provided in your answer book.

3. Insert today's date on letters and memos, unless otherwise instructed.

(Penalties will be incurred if these instructions are not followed.)

TSII-1 (Whitsun 1989 - 286)   © RSA 1989

Practise separating paragraphs by typing the following tasks:

Task 2

Use single-line spacing

British-made porcelain has always held a prominent place in the affections of connoisseurs. // However, over the last few decades production of specialities and hand-made items has been boosted by Royal occasions. // During the 1940s the industry was involved in large-scale production of utilities for the national war effort. //

Task 3

Type in double line spacing

Although farming has become a large and competitive industry, many market gardeners are still successful. // The current demand for organically-produced food has provided a further boost to many smallholders already involved in pick-your-own and Farm Shop activities. // None of these is exclusively suitable for market gardeners, but the large farm is often engaged in very different activities.

Space before and after headings

Leave at least one clear line before and after headings within the text. After a main heading at the top of a document it is common practice to leave an extra clear line. (N.B. Extra space after the main heading is always acceptable, even when an instruction is given to type the document in double-line spacing.)

```
10 July 1990

Our ref: S2A/C-O

Your ref: AGD/MD/1

Messrs Dickson & Derry
Merrydown Chambers
Merrydown Road
LEEDS   LS21 8TL

Dear Sirs

Monthly Sales
```

June	July	August
£	£	£
1000	900	610
241	1188	994

```
1. Never take stock later than
   15 March.

2. Always enter late items as
   'over'.

3. Do not enter any items
   beginning with '12'.
```

```
    We look forward to your
letter in due course.

    Your order has, in the
meantime, been processed.

Yours faithfully
```

PRAXITELES GROUP

A fictitious organisation for examination purposes only

PRAXITELES HOUSE · ADAM STREET · LONDON WC2N 6EZ
TELEPHONE 01 930 5115

Adjustment Invoice

Name and Address:

1

> Ledway Products Ltd
> Hillborough Works
> Beschings Street
> CHELMSFORD
> CM26 4HE

Invoice Date ....29 January 1990...........

2

Contract No ......DX/BEL/1/90.............

CONTRACT VALUE	ADJUSTMENTS + OR −	NETT	VAT RATE
£7106.60	+ £110.00	£6996.60	ZERO

Amount of contract   £ 6996.60

Deposit Paid   £ 2500

Value Added Tax   £ Nil

Balance   £

3   4996.60

Penalties incurred

`1 Overtyping of pre-printed material ⎤ *1 Accuracy Fault*
2 Overtyping of pre-printed material ⎦ *per line of entry*
3 Misaligned by at least one line space
   (*1 Presentation Fault*)

	Accuracy	Presentation
TOTAL FAULTS	2	1

Leaving space for the signature

It is good practice to adjust the amount of space to fit the signature of the person sending the letter. This is another example of the need, when working in an office, to adapt to different styles.

Because of the variations that are acceptable in real office work, you will not be penalised in the exam for the amount of space you leave for the signature in a letter. You **will** be penalised if you **fail** to leave **any** space at all for this purpose.

Other separate items

There are also many acceptable styles used in offices for showing which items are separate from others – for example, the date, the reference, the address, any special marks, and the opening of a letter ('salutation'). If you have an established work habit of leaving, say, two or three spaces after such items you may continue to do this in the exam.

PRACTICE MATERIAL
Practise separating items in the following tasks:

Task 4

RG 17 8XY

2 Queen Street Farnley, Berks. // (Today's date) // Mrs F E Thompson, 16 Hayforth Avenue, Wellington Downs, Durham. // Dear Mrs Thompson, // Thank you for your letter asking for a copy of my recipe for Honey and Almond Toffeecakes. // I understand Mary Johnson has published a book including this and other recipes from the area. The Toffee-cake recipe is included in a selection of items from her books to be printed next month. I have added your name and address to the mailing list. // Thank you for writing & for your interest. // Yours truly,

Complete the Adjustment Invoice to
Ledway Products Ltd Hillborough Works
Beschings Street CHELMSFORD CM26 4HE

Contract Value £7106.60   Inv. ~~Date~~ Date £ 29 Jan – 87
Adjustment   ✗ 110.00   Contract JX/BEL/1/87
Nett   6996.60 – Amount of Contract

    They pd deposit £2500 so balance ~~£4496.60~~
                                         £4496.60
       VAT NIL – ZERO RATE

Today's date

NOTICE // ALL STAFF ARE ENTITLED TO USE THE EMPLOYEES' DISCOUNT COUNTER // Simply obtain your Group Staff Identification Card from Personnel Office // There is no limit on the value of purchases you may make at 10% discount // Privilege Orders at Half Price are limited to nett cost of £200 per annum.

Task 6

FURNITURE PRICES

Item	Finish		Delivery
	Pine £	Yew £	
Dining Table	200	250	Ex Stock
Coffee Table	110	120	14 days
Dining Chair	67	72	Ex Stock
Sideboard	310	328	4 weeks
Desk	278	280	6 weeks
Dresser	242	268	8 weeks

C10   CORRECTIONS

Just as you practise and drill your keyboarding exercises in order to improve your skill, you also need to practise making corrections using a variety of materials and techniques. This will improve your skill in making corrections as inconspicuous as possible.

You must avoid:

1 **corrected characters appearing blurred or bold**.

a) Wait until fluid is dry.

b) Don't use too much pressure with an eraser so that the paper is left very thin and allows your corrections to be seen.

SCRIPT 2 – WORKED EXAMPLE

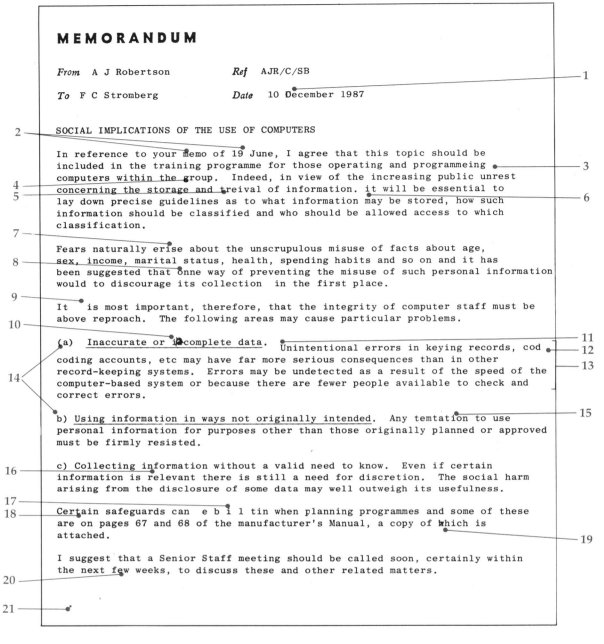

MEMORANDUM

From A J Robertson   *Ref* AJR/C/SB — 1

To F C Stromberg   *Date* 10 December 1987

2 — SOCIAL IMPLICATIONS OF THE USE OF COMPUTERS

In reference to your memo of 19 June, I agree that this topic should be
included in the training programme for those operating and programmeing — 3
computers within the group. Indeed, in view of the increasing public unrest
4 — concerning the storage and treival of information. it will be essential to — 6
5 — lay down precise guidelines as to what information may be stored, how such
information should be classified and who should be allowed access to which
classification.

7 — Fears naturally erise about the unscrupulous misuse of facts about age,
8 — sex, income, marital status, health, spending habits and so on and it has
been suggested that onne way of preventing the misuse of such personal information
would to discourage its collection in the first place.

9 — It   is most important, therefore, that the integrity of computer staff must be
10 — above reproach. The following areas may cause particular problems.

(a) Inaccurate or incomplete data. Unintentional errors in keying records, cod — 11, 12
coding accounts, etc may have far more serious consequences than in other — 13
14 — record-keeping systems. Errors may be undetected as a result of the speed of the
computer-based system or because there are fewer people available to check and
correct errors.

b) Using information in ways not originally intended. Any temtation to use — 15
personal information for purposes other than those originally planned or approved
must be firmly resisted.

16 — c) Collecting information without a valid need to know. Even if certain
information is relevant there is still a need for discretion. The social harm
arising from the disclosure of some data may well outweigh its usefulness.

17 — Certain safeguards can e b i l tin when planning programmes and some of these
18 — are on pages 67 and 68 of the manufacturer's Manual, a copy of which is — 19
attached.

I suggest that a Senior Staff meeting should be called soon, certainly within
20 — the next few weeks, to discuss these and other related matters.

21 —

Penalties incurred

1 Overtyping (*1 Accuracy Fault*)
2 Not as in draft (*1 Accuracy Fault each*)
3 Inaccurate word not amended (*1 Accuracy Fault*)
4 Non-essential capital letter not used as in draft (*1 Presentation Fault*)
5 Letters omitted from word (*1 Accuracy Fault*)
6 Incorrect character (*1 Accuracy Fault*)
7 Incorrect character in word (*1 Accuracy Fault*)
8 Additional character in word (*1 Accuracy Fault*)
9 More than two spaces following word (*1 Accuracy Fault*)
10 Handwritten insertion (*1 Accuracy Fault*)
11 Inconsistency in line spacing (*1 Presentation Fault*)

12 Additional word (*1 Accuracy Fault*)
13 Wording in wrong place (*1 Accuracy Fault*)
14 Inconsistency in presentation of lettered paragraphs (*1 Presentation Fault*)
15 Spelling error – letter omitted from word (*1 Accuracy Fault*)
16 Omission of underlining for emphasis as shown in draft (*1 Presentation Fault*)
17 Two words illegible (*2 Accuracy Faults*)
18 Word omitted (*1 Accuracy Fault*)
19 Overtyping (*1 Accuracy Fault*)
20 Incorrect word (*1 Accuracy Fault*)
21 Omission of indication of enclosure (*1 Accuracy Fault*)

	Accuracy	Presentation
TOTAL FAULTS	20	3

2 **the paper being left rough (smoothness impaired)**.

a) Don't use thick, lumpy fluid.

b) Don't rub so hard with an eraser that a rough, unsightly surface remains.

3 **hole(s) in the paper**.

a) If this occurs in a word, an Accuracy fault will be counted since a word, or part of a word, will be missing or illegible.

b) If a hole is made in a margin, or between paragraphs, you will receive a presentation fault.

4 **leaving character(s) illegible**.

a) Accuracy fault(s) will apply if corrected characters and/or those either side, above or below the correction are illegible.

b) Check your work carefully after correcting to make sure that this has not happened.

Correcting carbon copies

In Part 1 of the exam you will be required to make two carbon copies of one document.

If you correct carbon copies at the same time as correcting the top copy, **remember** to protect the copies while working on the top sheet (e.g. by inserting slips of paper or card behind carbon sheets). Equally important, **remember** to remove the protection slips after correcting your work.

Using self-correcting mechanisms

If your typewriter has a self-correcting mechanism, you may prefer to make corrections on carbon copies after the task is completed and removed from the machine. In this case, be careful to remove any excess carbon (use a soft eraser) before applying correcting fluid. When you re-insert each copy into the typewriter try to align the new, correct character(s) with the rest of the typing line, that is, produce a level line; but you will not be penalised for mis-alignment (on top copies or on carbon copies) unless character(s) are one-half line space or more above or below the original line.

Accuracy faults are not counted twice

Any errors already penalised on the top copy will not be penalised again in carbon copies. However, if you correct the top copy (no fault counted) but fail to correct the carbon copies, these errors will be counted as Accuracy faults (one fault only for each word not corrected in one or both copies).

- You are NOT expected to make INVISIBLE corrections, but your work should be USABLE in a real office by a DISCERNING EMPLOYER.

- PRACTICE is necessary for good correcting technique.

- DON'T RUSH! Go gently. Time for correcting is part of your rate of production.

From: A J Robertson to F C Stromberg.   Ref AJR/C/SB   *Memo*

SOCIAL IMPLICATIONS OF *THE* /USE OF COMPUTERS

In reference to your memorandum of 10 June, I agree that this topic should be included in the training programme for those operating and *programmeing* computers within the Group.   Indeed, in view of the increasing public unrest concerning the *retrieval and storage* of information, it will be essential to lay down precise guide lines as to what information may be stored, how such information should be classified and who should be allowed access to which classification.

Fears *arise naturally* about the unscrupulous misuse of facts about age, sex, income, marital status, health, spending habits and so on *xxxxxxxxxxxxx* and it has been suggested that one way of preventing the misuse of such personal information would be to discourage its collection in the first place.

It is most important, therefore, that the integrity of computer staff must be above reproach.   The following areas may cause particular problems.

(c) (a) *Innacurate* or incomplete data.   Unintentional errors in keying records, coding accounts, etc may have far more serious consequences than in other *index* record-keeping systems.   Errors may be undetected as a result of the speed of the computer-based system or because there are fewer people available to check and correct errors.   ~~Either way, considerable problems can occur as a result of apparently mistaken identity.~~

(a) (b) Collecting information without a valid need to know. Even if certain information is *relevent* there is still a need for discretion.   The social harm arising from the disclosure of some data may well outweigh its usefulness.

(b) (c) Using information in ways not originally intended. Any temptation to use personal information for purposes other than those originally planned or approved must be firmly resisted.

I suggest that a Senior Staff *m*/Meeting should be called soon, and certainly within the next two weeks, to discuss these and other related matters.

Certain safeguards can be built in when planning programmes and some of these are detailed on pages 67 and 68 of the manufacturer's *Manuel*, a copy of which is attached.

Section Three

The Part 1 Exam

8   *Rate of Production*

You must be able to work quickly enough to complete the three tasks:

- letter } on A4 printed stationery
- memo
- a piece of continuous text, e.g. an article or an extract from a report, on A4 or A5 paper.

Two carbon copies will be required, and you will have to address two labels.

GENERAL BUSINESS DOCUMENTATION

Part 1 is designed to show your competence in presenting general business documentation from drafts containing amendments.

Some of the amendments may be complicated and likely to cause confusion. **Read** carefully through before typing.

First-time accuracy takes less time than relying on corrections and retyping.

COPING WITH DISTRACTION

In a real office, few managers can arrange for typists to receive all their work at one time and to make sure the typist is not disturbed while working.

Only two of the three tasks in Part 1 will be given to you at the beginning of the exam. This allows you the chance to prove that you can concentrate and maintain your standards of work despite the distraction of knowing another task is to be issued for completion within the time allowed.

The third task will be placed on your desk by the invigilator between 15 and 30 minutes after the beginning of the exam. It will **not** be the longest of the three tasks, so you need not worry about having time to finish even if it is given to you half an hour after you begin typing.

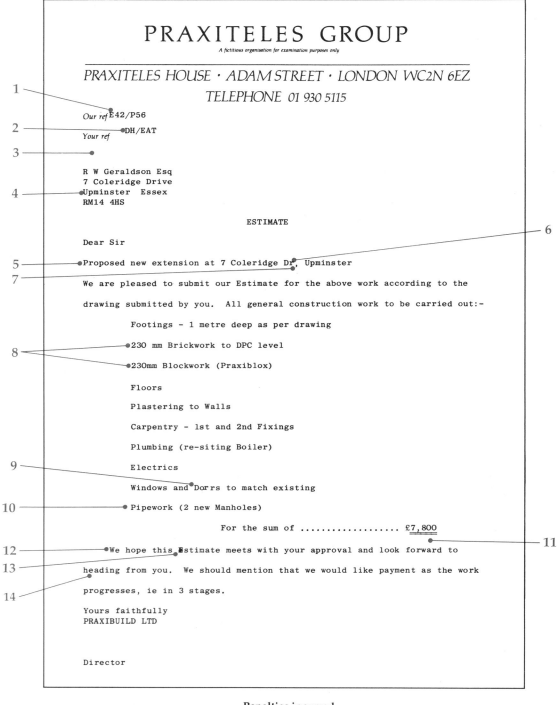

PRAXITELES GROUP

A fictitious organisation for examination purposes only

PRAXITELES HOUSE · ADAM STREET · LONDON WC2N 6EZ
TELEPHONE 01 930 5115

1 Our ref E42/P56

2 DH/EAT
   Your ref

3

R W Geraldson Esq
7 Coleridge Drive
4 Upminster Essex
RM14 4HS

ESTIMATE

Dear Sir

6

5 Proposed new extension at 7 Coleridge Dr, Upminster
7

We are pleased to submit our Estimate for the above work according to the

drawing submitted by you. All general construction work to be carried out:-

Footings - 1 metre deep as per drawing

230 mm Brickwork to DPC level
8
230mm Blockwork (Praxiblox)

Floors

Plastering to Walls

Carpentry - 1st and 2nd Fixings

Plumbing (re-siting Boiler)

9 Electrics

Windows and Dorrs to match existing

10 Pipework (2 new Manholes)

For the sum of £7,800

11

12 We hope this Estimate meets with your approval and look forward to
13
heading from you. We should mention that we would like payment as the work

14 progresses, ie in 3 stages.

Yours faithfully
PRAXIBUILD LTD

Director

Penalties incurred

1 No space after word 'ref' (*1 Accuracy Fault*)
2 Reference added by typist (who has no way of knowing its accuracy) (*1 Accuracy Fault*)

   Misaligned by at least one line space (*1 Presentation Fault*)
3 Date omitted (*3 Accuracy Faults*)
4 Capitals not used as shown in draft (*1 Presentation Fault*)
5 Capitals not used as shown in draft (*1 Presentation Fault*)
6 'Dr' not spelt in full (*1 Accuracy Fault*)
7 Inconsistency in style of punctuation: use of comma in contrast to open style used above (*1 Presentation Fault*)

8 Inconsistency in style of presenting abbreviations for measurement (*1 Presentation Fault*)
9 Keying error (*1 Accuracy Fault*)
10 Word in wrong place: amendment to text not incorporated (*1 Accuracy Fault*)
11 Two words omitted (*2 Accuracy Faults*)
12 Inconsistency in style of paragraphing (*1 Presentation Fault*)
13 Overtyping (*1 Accuracy Fault*)
14 Keying error (*1 Accuracy Fault*)

TOTAL	Accuracy	Presentation
FAULTS	12	6

IMPROVING YOUR RATE OF PRODUCTION

As well as keyboarding, correcting, setting-up and machine manipulation (see page 13), you should now drill and practise:

1 **assembling papers**

assembling and separating carbon sets consisting of

letterhead/memo form/plain ⎤
carbon paper   ⎟
flimsy paper   ⎬ This should take about 10 seconds.
carbon paper   ⎟
flimsy paper   ⎦

2 **inserting and straightening**

a) sets of paper and carbons;
b) small pieces of paper (labels).

3 **editing**

a) find given items throughout the draft for alteration.
b) read for meaning – find wrong words (mis-copying) as well as wrong characters (mis-keying) in your own work and in circled words in drafts (see syllabus item B9 on page 48).
c) scanning, reading, interpreting drafts.

4 **organising time and materials**

a) arrange your working area to help you feel like a professional, not an amateur.
b) work smoothly and fluently.
c) make sure you don't lose track of time.

5 **spelling**

Learn the words which may be shortened in drafts for you to spell the full word (see syllabus item B4 on page 5).

CHECK YOUR PROGRESS

You may be able to complete some types of task more quickly than others, so it is important to time yourself over all three tasks in Part 1 of the exam.

To help you to do this, the book includes timed exam practice for Part 1 on pages 53–55. It consists of three typical Part 1 exam tasks with target completion times. The two specimen Stage II papers in Section Five will also give you the opportunity to time your production rate as you complete the tasks in Part 1.

By filling in the progress record – included in the stationery section at the back of the book – you will be able to monitor your progress as you complete each set of three tasks.

Section Five

Exam Practice

14 *Examples of Three Marked
Exam Scripts and
Two Specimen Exam Papers*

SCRIPT 1 – EXAM TASK

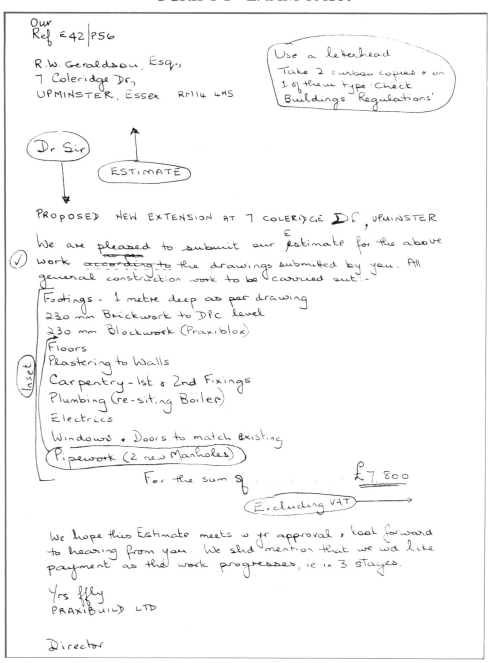

Our
Ref E42/P56

R.W. Geraldson, Esq.,
7 Coleridge Dr,
UPMINSTER, Essex RM114 4HS

Use a letterhead
Take 2 carbon copies & on
1 of them type 'Check
Buildings Regulations'

Dr Sir

ESTIMATE

PROPOSED NEW EXTENSION AT 7 COLERIDGE Dr, UPMINSTER

We are pleased to submit our estimate for the above
work according to the drawings submitted by you. All
general construction work to be carried out:-

Footings - 1 metre deep as per drawing
230 mm Brickwork to DPC level
230 mm Blockwork (Praxiblox)
Floors
Plastering to Walls
Carpentry - 1st & 2nd Fixings
Plumbing (re-siting Boiler)
Electrics
Windows & Doors to match existing
Pipework (2 new Manholes)

Inset

For the sum of £7,800
Excluding VAT

We hope this Estimate meets w yr approval & look forward
to hearing from you. We shd mention that we wd like
payment as the work progresses, ie in 3 stages.

Yrs ffly
PRAXIBUILD LTD

Director

B1 DATES

All letters and memos must be dated. Unless you are given instructions to the contrary, this will be the date on which the work is typed.

In a real office, other documents may also require a date, and this is part of the information that you will need to find out when starting an office job. In the exam you will be given instructions, or the date will be shown, if it is required in any document other than the letter or memo.

Style

It is **not** generally accepted practice for the day or the year in a document date to be typed in words like this:

The fifteenth of January nineteen hundred and ninety

If a date is specially written in for you to copy there is no need to change the style used by the writer, but you will not be penalised for doing so – so long as the **correct** date is inserted.

When it is left to you to provide the date for the letter or memo you may type it in the style you normally use, that is, day–month–year, month–day–year.

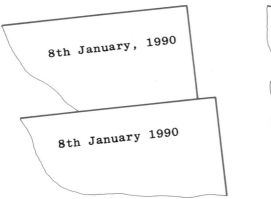
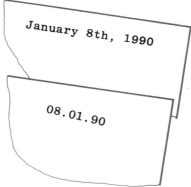

DATES IN FIGURES

You should be wary of using all figures for the date unless you have a good reason for doing so. This is because all-figure dates can cause confusion in real-life use. For example:

2.1.90 may mean '2 January 1990'

but Continental and American ways of reading and writing dates are becoming more common in the UK (particularly because of the increasing use of imported computer software), and in these styles

2.1.90 means 'February 1 1990'

There are, of course, some offices where all-figure dates are the house style and where all concerned clearly understand the style and in the exam you will not be penalised if you type the correct date in figures.

Task 67

Complete in Enquiry Form to be sent to Allied Warehousing Ltd, Industrial Park, Telford TF14 9EY for

Storage of 24 Desks 1200mm x 900mm x 1000mm high
24 Swivel Armchairs
16 Four-drawer Filing Cabinets
5 Hat/Coat Stands

for a period of 6 months (minimum)

For attention of Jamil Putrah. Sent by Contracts Dept
Date today

Task 68

Type on Order Form No. DET/16892 dated today, to
James Garden Products Ltd
Summervale Estate
TIPPINGTON
Essex IG7 4TB

For delivery to Praci Gardening + Estates
Branitent Works   BRANITENT
Sheridon Row
BLACKBURN BB21 0XY

4 Wooden Benches Cat No D/604
12 Wooden Half-Tubs Cat No R/16
10 Bird Tables   FE/47
4 Garden Tables   WA/G21

The goods are required as soon as possible + the order will be signed by a Clerk in the Furniture Department.

Date as a separate item

The document date has to be shown as a separate item, with at least one clear line space before and after it, so that it can be quickly and easily seen (see syllabus item C9 (e)).

In some cases, however, the writer may indicate that no space is required when the date is included with other details e.g. at the foot of a report of a similar item:

i.e.   to be typed as:

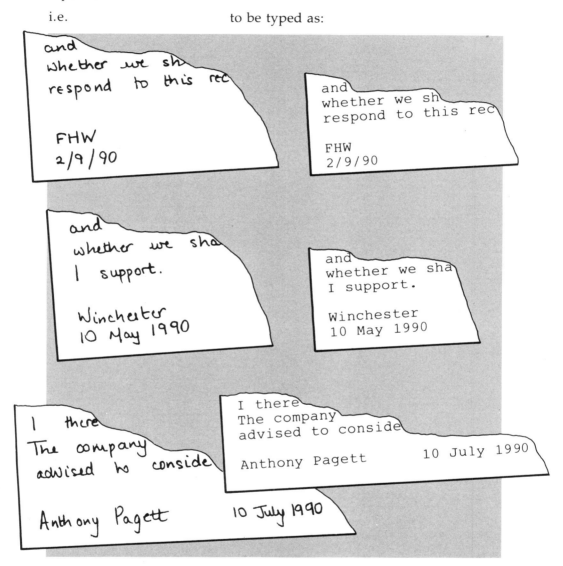

You should always attempt to follow the layout shown in the draft for special cases. The writer may use a style that you have not used or seen before. This should not stop you from following any instructions, given explicitly or clearly implied.

Post-dating

In addition to the normal procedure of dating documents with the day on which they are typed, you will be required, in Part 1 of the exam, to work out and insert the date for a day up to two weeks ahead.

Use the Remittance Advice Form to advise the
following payments to E J Hayes Ltd 29 Barrings Row,
Southall, Middx UB10 7LXB: (List the items in date order)

Nov	Invoice	
1	62894	114.92
9	63990	210.60
3	Ax/41T	36.90
16	86887	410.80
Dec		
7	111/6BC	22.18
4	8/T	1.10
12	8G742	150.45
		£946.95

paid by credit transfer
through bank

Complete an Action List for Administration Sector,
for the period 2 weeks from Monday of next week to
Friday of the following week (enter dates only).

Contract Ref: Studley House	Complete 4th Floor Construction Electrical Wiring to Floors 2 + 3 Fixtures & Fittings to Floor 1	J D Harper Brenda Howes Fay Jarles
Contract Job 68418	Steering Group meeting. Papers to be despatched 7 days in advance	Jean Colley
Davidson Dawes & Co	Project outline required for in 3 weeks To be issued today to Supervisors & Operatives	Kevin Wells

Complete a Job List for week after next (give date of the Friday)
Sheet 1 of 1 for the following Jobs for Reprography Department:

1000	copies of Course T/104B for	James Tobie
500	Price Lists - Electronic Goods -	AAT/ A D Halleys
2500	Standard Letterheads -	Stationery Stores
250	Students Handbook	D Crowe, Science Faculty
1600	Requisition Forms	Stationery Stores
100	Catalogue p.27	Post Room

Enter items in descending order of quantity

> Dear Mrs Boult
>
> Thank you for your letter. My secretary has now made an appointment, as suggested, for Tuesday of next week (insert the date) at 10.30 am. I look forward to meeting you & will bring all of the relevant documents

The date asked for will always be for a specific day, e.g. 'the first Thursday of next month' or 'Tuesday of the week after next'; *not* 'next Wednesday' (if the exam were on a Tuesday you might worry whether this meant the next day or Wednesday of the following week).

YOU NEED TO:

- know today's date;

- know how many days in the month (in case the date you have to give is after the end of the month);

- count the days and dates accurately.

PRACTICE MATERIAL

Practise post-dating in each of the following tasks:

Task 7

> From J A Maching
> To Penny Archer
> Today's date
>
> (Type a note on plain paper)
>
> Ferrydown Printers telephoned today. I told them Mr Jones to ring you by Thursday of next week (give date) so as to give you time to meet the Budget deadlines.   JAM

Task 8

> (Please type this)
> Extract from my notes for the meeting on Tuesday
>
> The Committee will be pleased to know that the Regional Association of Leisure Clubs met on (give day & date for the last day of last month) and approved the plans for the new Clubhouse at Farnworth.

In Tasks 62 to 68 practice:

a) setting up margin and tab stops;
b) sorting given information;
c) typing on pre-printed forms;
d) checking (and correcting where necessary) your entries;
e) checking the date: insert date of typing in the absence of instruction.

Aim to complete all of the above for each form within a maximum of 20 minutes each time.

Task 62

Use the Quotation Form (at the back of the book). Enter the following details

To Ledway Fortiweg Ltd 29 Balderton Way Nottingham
NG27 42YB

Your Ref 107/
AX

120 litres Timbercare £359.15
130 litres Shell Rose Vinyl finish £370.22

Carrige: Collect
Dely date: 14 days from order
Terms: Nett   From Special Contracts Division
Today's date

Task 63

Type an Order Form as follows:
2 Tabulatory desks
14 Special fixings for Tabulatory desk drawers
9 Trays for Tabulatory inserts
18 Tabulatory Triangles
2 chairs - design 'Tabulatory'
        for delivery by 21 next month to our address

Order No 628431 dated today to be signed in INDENTS
Goods to be ordered from: TREDINGTON FURNITURE CO Dept.
                                                unit 4
Change 'Tabulatory'   Belvedere Trading Estate
to 'Disctable' throughout   caps -Warrington WA14 32TB

RSA Typewriting Skills Book Two   Part 2: Presentation

Type a letter on plain paper

116 Fenchurch Road
Werrybank Road
Dudley
West Midlands
DY38 14TU

Use today's date

Messrs Baines & Grace
Charity Chambers
Denwell Grove
OAKWORTH   West Yorkshire
BD41 1ZU

Dear Sirs

Your last letter promised the final documentation for my house purchase. This is now extremely urgent, as the present occupiers need to have everything settled by (give date for the last day of next month). This sounds plenty of time but in order to comply, I need the documents for financial arrangements to be started no later than (give date for Friday of the week after next).

Yours faithfully

B2   LOCATING INFORMATION

Most office tasks are linked with at least one other job, or document, using or conveying the same details. It is not always convenient to wait until the documents incorporating the same information are all drafted before passing them to the typist at one time.

One of the qualities that distinguishes the reliable typist from the beginner is the ability to find and to transfer information from one task to another. This means that tasks containing information required for jobs still being prepared by the executive can be passed to the typist, who can start work on the completed drafts and then be asked to transfer details to the new tasks when they are received.

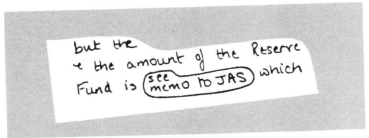

but the
r the amount of the Reserve Fund is (see memo to JAS) which

In Part 1 of the exam you will have to locate information in either Task 1 or Task 2 for inclusion in Task 3, which is issued to you after the exam has begun.

2 Sequencing of details

The information for entry is not always given in the same order as the headings appear on the form:

PRAXITELES GROUP
A fictitious organisation for examination purposes only

PRAXITELES HOUSE · ADAM STREET · LONDON WC2N 6EZ
TELEPHONE 01 930 5115

Our ref

Your ref

QUOTATION

Dear Sirs

We are pleased to quote as follows:

Item	Ref. No.	Price	Delivery date

Terms ....   Carriage ....

We look forward to receipt of your order.

Yours faithfully

*Sales Enquiries Department / Special Contracts Division

*Delete as appropriate

Complete Quotation
for 112 litres yellow Paint
                    Ref No 1102
Our ref: JB/692
from Sales Enquiries Dept
£262.12   carr. paid
Terms Nett
Dely Date 12 Nov next
To Lucas Fendy Ltd
    12 Priony Street
    Lindhon LN2 4BT

In this case, it is particularly important to mark items which must be entered against separate headings or in a particular place, for example, the address on the quotation. In addition, you may need a reminder to make a deletion: in the details above 'from Sales Enquiries Department' means you must delete 'Special Contracts Division' on the form.

3 Unfamiliar words

Forms are another type of task in which product names often occur, as well as names and addresses. All of these will be double-checked by you when you are in a real office job. In the exam you cannot ask, and in any case these details have to be fictitious. So remember: copy exactly any foreign or unfamiliar words appearing in the draft.

WENTWORTH ESTATES

Item No.	Property	Price
1	House 1-bed	£50,000
2	Bungalow	83,000
3	House 5-bed	200,000
4	Mews Cott.	215,000
5	Flat 2-bed	61,000
6	House	77,500

Dear Mrs Clark

The vendors now confirm the listed price of 12 Victoria Close as

(Item 6 on list)

Your lower offer is therefore unacceptable at present & we shall be glad of your further instructions

Yours faithfully
WENTWORTH ESTATES

The information to be located will be one single item only, that is, a sum of money, a date, a name, address, etc.

- INFORMATION IS REQUIRED for Task 3.
- ONLY ONE ITEM needs to be found.
- LOCATE the details in Task 1 or Task 2.

PRACTICE MATERIAL

In the following exercises practise:

a) remembering to include the date of typing;
b) post-dating;
c) locating information.

Task 10

Mrs Ann JENTISS
Policy No HA#21683×D
Jaguar XJ

Type a note on plain paper to J C Denkin, Motor Accounts Dept

Mrs Jentiss called in to collect her Certificate of Insurance. She wanted me to be sure you know she is on holiday from 12 August to Sept 9.

Is your 'phone out of order? Am getting this typed so the typist will remember to check it with you after I leave for Bristol (in 5 minutes' time). See you next Wednesday in the Brandling Hotel.   MWT

C14 COMPLETING FORMS

Most office jobs involve working with a variety of forms. Letterheads and memos are forms in which you have to align typing with pre-printed headings, for example, 'Your ref, Date, To, From'.

Other forms have boxes, lines and vertical rulings, which also involve the typist in aligning entries, setting up margins and tab stops and repeated checking to make sure that typing is properly aligned throughout the form.

At first sight, it seems easy to see where details should be entered on a form, but there are some pitfalls and common errors.

1 *Separate headings*

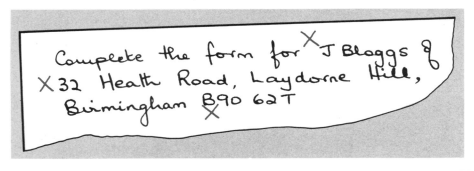

To avoid the above, take time before putting the form into the typewriter to mark the items that have their own separate heading:

16 Highgate
Densling Chark
MANSTOWE
Cornwall
CM3 8ST

The Manager
Brandling Hotel
The Downings (DOWNINGS)
BRISTOL BS21 8TL

Dear Sir/Madam

This is to confirm reservation of 2 single rooms from (date for Wed. of next week) to (Tued of week after next) for myself and Mr John E Denkin. I understand one room with bath will be available from (first date) but that a second room with bath will not be available until the Friday (give date) + in the meantime the second room will be on the third floor.

We expect to arrive by 9 pm on Wednesday (date).

Yours faithfully

M. W. THOMAS (Miss)

(Note on plain paper to Steven)

Steve

Sorry I didn't see you before I left for Bristol. Shall be at the Woodbram Hotel, 12 Charr Street until Wed (give date) when moving to the Brandling Hotel (give address).

Will phone in at least every other day. Hope the Anderson account goes well.

MWT

(Type me a letter to my plumber)

16 High ———
D ——— c ———
m ———
c ———
CM3 8ST

Mr R Ashton
25 Barley Heights
MANSTOWE CM3 8PA

Dear Ray

Thanks for your bill. As agreed, we'll settle all the accounts together at the end of next month.

I promised to let you know date of my return from Bristol. I shall be leaving the Brandling H——— on (give date).

Any date after then will be suitable to me for you to install the shower.

Sincerely

Time allowed:
Preparation   5 mins
Typing   15 mins
Checking/correcting   5 mins
                25 mins

Task 61

(Circled note: Use L'ayout as shown for Item 4 — para + heading)

MINUTES of Meeting of Directors held at Gooche House on Tuesday 10 November

Present: E A Henshaw (Chair)
D A Holmes
F G Parsons
D J Denks
D Appleby
B Chartwelle

(Circled note: Type in alpha order Do not type bracket)

In attendance: K Welling (Secretary to the meeting) and T Sorreson (Registrar)

1. Apologies - None received

2. Minutes - Confirmed & signed by Chair

3. Matters Arising - There were none two: had been made.
   Minute 8 - No progress Dokot's report was due in 2 weeks.
   Minute 9 - Miss

4. PROCEDURES BOOKLET
   The booklet ref PRO/5/86 (i) was received. Several minor amendments were made (see Minute Book).

   Chair expressed thanks to all those concerned in its production.

5. Training Courses. These had been well-received and so many people had wanted to attend that waiting lists had been created.
   The allocation of revenue for last year's courses had now been exhausted and it was agreed that to a 10% increase in the allocation for this year.
   (margin note: allocate / recommend)
   The courses run last year should be repeated. In addition, 3 new courses were approved as follow-on for staff who had attended last year.

6. NEXT MEETING
   Two dates were agreed: 4 March and 4 July.

There being no other business, the meeting closed at 4.30 pm.

B3 AMENDMENTS TO TEXT

Shown in the exam as: Indicating:

In coffee plantations ...

We are required ...

items crossed out and
replaced by other words

items crossed out
without replacement

These amendments are included in every exam, just as they may be a
normal part of any work prepared for final typing. If you train yourself to
expect them, and recognise that it is part of your skill to take account of
them, you won't be 'put off' by the appearance of edited work.

The exam will also include these signs:

Shown in the exam as: Indicating:

Of course, not everyone
likes justified text, and
for some purposes it
looks too formal. || To
switch off justification,
press CTRL f3 -
JUSTIFICATION.

The letter J to the
left of the ruler at
the top of the screen
disappears.

start a new paragraph here //

or [

no new paragraph here

To be typed as:

```
Of course, not everyone likes justified text, and for some purposes
it looks too formal.

To switch off justification, press CTRL f3 - JUSTIFICATION.  The letter
J to the left of the ruler at the top of the screen disappears.
```

Task 60

Time allowed:
Reading/marking 5 mins
Typing 15 mins
Checking/correcting 5 mins
25 mins

CHARNFORTH BUILDINGS PLC

REPORT ON MEETING OF PRODUCTION MANAGERS
held on 29 October

Item ~~Present~~	~~Proceedings~~	~~Action~~
Scheme 6	After further consideration it was agreed to allocate £5000.	FGP
Deferred Scheme 4	It was agreed this Scheme was no longer applicable & shd be dropped from future Agendas.	Secretary
Site 8	No agreement was reached on Contract 48/ALS for Saunders. The ~~matter~~ Steel still requires further information & has referred the item back	Site Manager, AEB

Scheme 2 ~~also~~ deferred No further details being available, this was deferred, & referred back - Action Bill Mays

Site 14 This was fully discussed, including allocations and staffing. Mr Levings was appointed Deputy Site Manager, and Frank Hudson agreed to arrange manning levels from next month. Action FH

Barringtons Breakdown reports were read regarding Drum Pourer No 444. These showed deficiencies were due to wear & tear. It was agreed to apply for replacement as soon as possible. Action HEB

Hamish Completion date was notified. Frank Hudson agreed to raise manning levels and transfer hands to comply. Action FH

Meeting Dates Group agreed to hold meetings first Monday of each month. Action-Secretary

TYPIST: Type in 3 columns and rule, as shown for first 3 items.
Change 'Scheme' to 'Site' throughout

Here are seven more signs that may be used in the exam:

Shown in the exam as: Indicating:

We are ^not^ ~~sorry~~ ...	We are not sorry ...	insert letter(s) or word(s) here
He was taken (only) .	Only he was taken.	insert or move word(s) to here (as arrowed)
Among (a few) many.	A few among many.	change places
12 / 10 24 / 20 36 / 30	10 20 30 12 24 36	change places
Bat teries	Batteries	leave no space
First class	First class	put in space
✓ We have ~~no~~ ^many^ doubts.	We have no doubts.	include word(s) or figure(s) crossed out

No **other** amendment or correction signs will be included.

Take care!

Amendments look quite simple when shown separately as in this book, or in a straightforward style in tasks. However, they can be used in much more complicated ways, and it is sometimes necessary to look very carefully to be sure you type the right words in the right order.

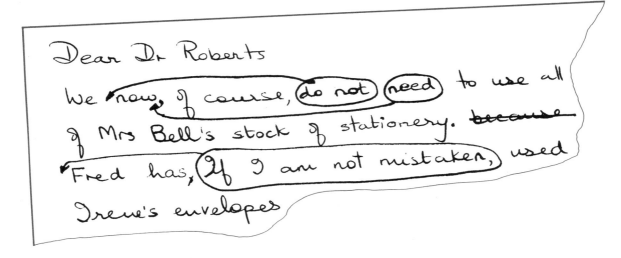

When documents must be typed to rigid requirements, details of format will be given to you: such **precise** positioning is rare in office work, but it is important on many occasions that a **general** layout is followed carefully as in the following example:

```
                    REPORT on the meeting held on

                    22nd August 1987 between James

                    Taylor and Elvyn Woods at the

                    offices of Jenkins Melbing Ltd

Presented documents included the Will of Mr Edmund
```

While it is not important for the heading to begin at one precise point (for instance, 45, 48, 50 spaces from left edge of paper), it is **very** important that the general layout should be followed, that is, the heading must be clearly to the right and in double-line spacing in order to set it apart from the body of the text below.

Specific requirements

You may well be asked to type documents and layouts that are new to you; or perhaps to present familiar documents with layouts quite different from those you have previously used.

Before starting to type, you need to analyse what is required and which facilities of your machine will be useful for the job.

When using different layouts from your usual style, it is very easy to slip back into your own routine – so don't rely on your memory! It is safer and quicker to mark the draft with the modifications to be made.

■ FOLLOW general instructions carefully, but you can make your own decisions about specific detail.

■ USE YOUR PENCIL – a note written down is worth two in the mind!

■ USE YOUR MACHINE FACILITIES to work quickly and effectively.

In the exam, instructions may refer to more than one way in which layout is to be modified:

```
Steel Sheets        Platinum
Mild Steel Rods     Silver          Divide into three
Pig Iron            Copper          columns & type in
                                    double-line spacing.
```

You will incur one presentation fault for every modification not carried out as instructed.

This should be typed as:

Dear Dr Roberts

We do not now need, of course, to use all of Mrs Bell's stock
of stationery. If I am not mistaken, Fred has used Irene's
envelopes ...

Typing from edited drafts is not difficult, but you may find it tedious.
Always work carefully and calmly to make sure that what is really a
simple job, well within your ability, does not cause you unnecessary
penalties.

- ■ TYPISTS OFTEN FORGET to include
  – the rest of the original sentence after an amendment.
  – punctuation in an amendment.

- ■ BE PATIENT!

PRACTICE MATERIAL

Task 14   Practise finding and transferring information in the following tasks: **Task 15**

The lack of provision of Stock
Leaflets in the Post Room is often
the cause of delay in replying
to Customer Initial Enquiries.

1 Post Room staff must adhere
strictly to the re-ordering
procedure. || Supervisors must
ensure minimum stock levels
are still appropriate in view of
current requirements and
commitments.

2. Reprography Room staff
must not disregard Priority
Grades given to Leaflet
orders by Supervisors.

NOTICE

EAB
21/4/90

TO ALL SUPERVISORS

C — I — E — are the single
most important source of our
sales orders. out It is essential
they shd receive attention
promptly # Any delay can result
in loss of orders, which,

This wastes money spent on
newspaper advertisements. Bottlenecks seem to occur from time
to time through the Post Room
because
runs. out of stocks of Stock
Leaflets.

general
I have sent a note to all
Post Room & Reprography staff
but shall be glad if you will keep
an eye on this & check if there
are other sources of delay.

EAB
21/4/90

RSA Typewriting Skills Book Two   Part 1: Accuracy

C13 MODIFYING LAYOUT

In real office work, instructions regarding change of layout are often given in vague terms, such as 'Move this column to the left of that column' or 'Reverse the order of these two sections and use the headings as column 1'. Managers who give general instructions in this way rely on the typist to decide on how they should be implemented.

In any of the tasks in Part 2 of the exam you may be instructed to move items, change style of presentation, or to make other modification(s) affecting the layout of the material. Follow the instructions carefully:

To be typed as:

1. Brandy Snaps - Available in stock in 3 kilo cartons £7.90	1. BRANDY SNAPS Available in stock in 3 kilo cartons. £7.90
2. ALLSORTS Not a stock item. To be ordered in boxes for direct delivery £6.84	2. ALLSORTS Not a stock item. To be ordered in boxes for direct delivery. £6.84
3. Jelly Babies: Ex stock in 3 kilo cartons of mixed flavours. £6.50	3. JELLY BABIES Ex stock in 3 kilo cartons of mixed flavours. £6.50

Type all headings as No. 2 & type each price on separate line at left margin

If you had typed the example above, you might have chosen to type the prices on the **next** separate line, instead of leaving a clear line space. This would be acceptable, because you would have complied with the general instruction, and the specific detail of the way in which you carry out general instructions can be a matter of your choice. However, you should have typed the headings as shown in the draft because you were given a specific model to copy.

Following general layout

The ability to follow copy is important for a typist. Many offices have their own style for particular documents, the 'house style', and you will be expected to be able to copy layouts without detailed explanations.

Interim Report to General Manager
Ms Julie H Evershed,

Please type in double
line spacing, on plain
paper

In response to your request for investigation of delays:

1. Customer In—— E—— seem to be delayed by lack of stock lists in the Post Room. Staff in the Post Room and the Rep—— Room have been asked to strictly adhere to existing procedures.

2. Copy for the Annual R—— & A—— should now be available one month prior to p—— date. One cause of delay in the past would was copy held up for final Sales figures. Mr J—— has now agreed to accept copy from today & to insert such figures when they are available.

EAB
Today's date

DRAFT
Annual Report & Accounts

Type on Plain Paper
in double line spacing

We are being asked by our printers to ensure that all copy for this year's Report & Accounts booklet is available for by at least one month prior to publication date. [We are constantly pressed on such matters but I shall be glad if everyone will ensure they he/she is are not the cause of delay on this occasion].

NOTICE

A—— R—— & A——

Publication date is 22 July. All copy must be available for our printers by 22 J—— at the latest. // All staff responsible for producing figures, paragraphs, illustrations & tables should note that Mr P D Jamieson will accept drafts from today. // Do not delay completion of drafts by waiting for final Sales figures. These will be inserted by Mr Jamieson.

Time allowed:
Planning   3 mins
Typing   15 mins
Checking/correcting   5 mins
              23 mins

(Today's date)

Re-arrange in order of price, starting at highest price

42 Steyning Crescent

3 Bedrooms, Large living-room, separate kitchen 12 ft x 18 ft. Gardens to front and rear £23,000

116 Parkhill Lane

3 Bedrooms, 2 reception rooms, kitchen 10 ft x 15 ft. Garage, gardens to (rear and front) £25,000

27 Nymorning Lane

2 bedrooms, large living/kitchen on ground floor, large garden to rear. Planning permission for renovation and some extension £12,950

38 Flet Road

4 Bedrooms including loft conversion, 3 good reception rooms including dining/kitchen. Central heating. Garage £24,500
       12 ft x 16 ft.

47 Tichill

3 bedrooms, bathroom with shower, separate toilet. 2 large reception rooms, open plan kitchen/dining room, waste disposal unit. Central heating and double glazing throughout. Separate brick garage £41,000

79 Great Moor

5 bedrooms, one with bathroom en suite, dressing-room. Bathroom, shower room and toilet each (separate). 4 receptions rooms, large, and kitchen fully fitted. Utility room. (Garage.) (Impeccable gardens) Double Glazing and Central Heating throughout. £78,500

B4 SPELLING

a) Spelling words accurately

As a typist, words are your stock-in-trade. At the very least, you should note spellings and what types of word must be grouped together to make proper sentences. Otherwise you will make mistakes and not be able to spot errors.

You cannot expect to know how to spell every word, but it is your responsibility to care enough to **check** that your work is accurate.

CHECKING WORK

The syllabus tests spelling by shortening words in the draft. You will be expected to type in full any of the words listed on pages 5 – 6. In the exam the first few letters of a shortened word will help you check its spelling in a dictionary.

PHRASES

As well as single words shortened for you to spell in full, three abbreviations of phrases are included in the list on page 5, i.e.

f/t (full time)
p/t (part time)
asap (as soon as possible)

> We bel cos dev the exp of resp staff
> by sending them on p/t courses.
>
> We believe companies develop the experience of responsible
> staff by sending them on part time courses.

In most offices there are phrases, as well as single words, which are used so often that writers abbreviate them and rely on typists to spell out the word(s) in full. These may be technical terms related to a particular business, or short cuts favoured by individuals. For example; 'f/t' and 'p/t' will be used frequently in personnel offices when referring to types of worker, or in colleges where students are on full or part-time courses. 'Asap' and 'info' are typical of abbreviations used often by some people but rarely by others.

In real life you need to find out the abbreviations that may be used by different writers. The list on pages 5 – 6 shows you the abbreviations that may be used in the exam.

READING FOR SENSE

Some of the abbreviations of words for spelling can represent more than one word, e.g. 'rec' could be used for 'receipt' or 'receive'. Only by **reading** the sentence in which the abbreviation appears can you decide which word you need.

Practise your routine for rearranging items before typing, so that you can complete Tasks 57–59 within the time allowances suggested. Remember to check your work for accuracy. Note: timings refer to preparation as well as keying and checking.

Task 57

Time allowed:
Preparation	*10 mins*
Typing	*12 mins*
Checking/correcting	*5 mins*
	27 mins

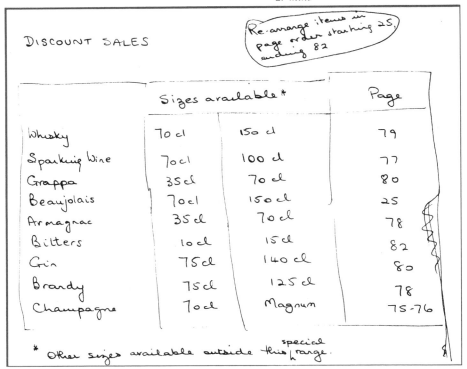

DISCOUNT SALES

Re-arrange items in page order starting 25, ending 82

	Sizes available *		Page
Whisky	70 cl	150 cl	79
Sparkling Wine	70 cl	100 cl	77
Grappa	35 cl	70 cl	80
Beaujolais	70 cl	150 cl	25
Armagnac	35 cl	70 cl	78
Bitters	10 cl	15 cl	82
Gin	75 cl	140 cl	80
Brandy	75 cl	125 cl	78
Champagne	70 cl	Magnum	75-76

* Other sizes available outside this special range.

Task 58

Time allowed:
Planning	*7 mins*
Typing	*15 mins*
Checking/correcting	*5 mins*
	27 mins

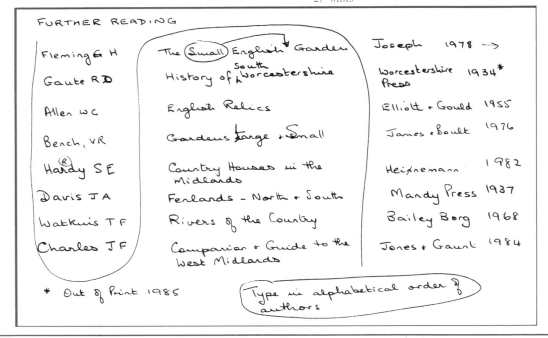

FURTHER READING

Fleming G H	The (Small) English Garden	Joseph 1978 →
Gaute R D	History of South Worcestershire	Worcestershire Press 1934 *
Allen WC	English Relics	Elliott + Gould 1955
Bench, VR	Gardens Large + Small	James + Boult 1976
Hardy S E	Country Houses in the Midlands	Heinemann 1982
Davis JA	Fenlands - North + South	Mandy Press 1937
Watkins TF	Rivers of the Country	Bailey Borg 1968
Charles JF	Companion + Guide to the West Midlands	Jones + Gaunt 1984

* Out of Print 1985

Type in alphabetical order of authors

We have recd yt payment & you wl rec a rec in the next few days.

We have received your payment and you will receive a receipt in the next few days.

PRACTICE MATERIAL

Type the following tasks, check your work, then make corrections as necessary.

Task 19

Costing (Type in double linespacing)

We have to take a/c of the has of work wh many people devote to designing bus cats. The org has to balance weight the total costs of producing these documents peoples time against the advantages gained thro' their publication. // Printing and distribution a/c for costs are only a proportion of the costs. It is easy to overlook the exp of modelling our the clothes, collecting & arranging info about them, photography and other activities wh may at first sight appear to be sep activities but wh are really have to be ack as part of the designer's work.

Task 20

The Finance and General Purposes Cttee have has agreed to recom the following pay increases with immed effect:-

Typists	5%	Bar Checkers	7%
Counter Clerks	4%	Machine Operators	4%

Temp staff wl be included in the plan asap. P/t workers wl not be rec awards this yr, having recd approx 6% increases in 1988 & 1989. // Work is proceeding on a plan to gntee work for both temp & P/t employees in misc departments.

C12   REARRANGING ITEMS

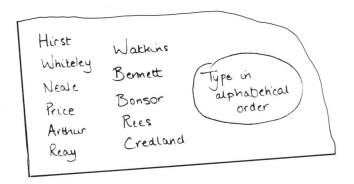

Simple routine

1 **Count** items to be rearranged (eleven in the example above).

2 **Number** items on the draft, in order for typing:

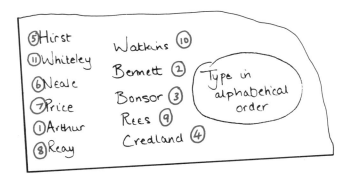

3 **Check** your numbering tallies with your **count** (eleven).

4 **Type**, and **tick** each item when completed.

5 **Count** your final typed list to make sure all (eleven) are included.

   Practise this routine; set yourself time targets for the **count/number/ check** part of the routine, that is, before you start typing. **Remember**, it is easy to overrun your time in the exam by taking too long to think, analyse and sort.

- Errors in carrying out general instructions to REARRANGE incur penalties for PRESENTATION.

- Errors in WORDS incur ACCURACY penalties.

- FOLLOW A ROUTINE
  - COUNT
  - NUMBER AND CHECK
  - TYPE AND TICK
  - COUNT AGAIN

b) *Abbreviations to be retained*

Bros	Ltd	plc	Co	NB	eg	etc	viz
Mrs	Miss	Ms	Mr	Dr	MP	Rev	JP

All of the above are examples of abbreviations which must not be altered or spelt in full. A number of these abbreviations will be included in Part 1 of the exam.

In addition, the abbreviation '&' may be used in names of organisations, when it should not be altered or spelt out (although the handwritten sign for 'and' in sentences must, of course, be typed in full).

e.g.   To be typed as:

Joan and I have an appointment with

Dobbs & Co and we expect to meet

Mr Jones and Mrs Feech who works for

Filty & Barnes Ltd.

- ■ MAKE SURE YOU KNOW MEANINGS as well as spellings of the words listed in syllabus item B4(a) (see pages 5–6).

- ■ COPY other abbreviations such as those in syllabus item B4(b) (see page 6).

PRACTICE MATERIAL

Type the following tasks, taking care to retain abbreviations that must not be spelt in full:

Task 21

MEMORANDUM

From Barry Jones   *Ref*   (Use a memo form.)

To Mavis Dankey   today's *Date*

FULMAN & FORTY PRODUCTS (PTY) — ORDER NO 6824

We have today recd the contract wh covers bulk deliveries, & the above order can now be released for production.

Incidentally, we are releasing space on ~~As a matter of interest,~~ MV "HOPEAWAY" sailing on 10th of next month from London. It may be that ~~this~~ Darby & Co can reallocate the to Order 6824. ~~providing you can contact them today.~~ Alternatively

Fulman & Forty have now confirmed ~~informed~~ that their handling agents for USA wl be JENNY PRODUCTS INC.

Extract from Page 16 of the summer catalogue, showing amendments required on re-printing

Goods are supplied on condition that should they not be as required[1] goods may be returned to us using the pre-paid labels attached to the Order Pack.[2]

Full details of the
a) goods ordered and
b) goods despatched
must be entered on Form 612A, also part of the Order Pack.

Should goods be despatched as ordered but not to found to be suitable by the customer, ~~Order~~ Form 824A should be completed showing
a) full catalogue details
b) reason for return
c) alternative catalogue item required
   OR
d) value of goods for cash refund.

Customers completing d) above should also indicate whether if a Post Office Giro Cheque is required. ~~or if they have a bank account,~~ Customers holding current bank account should enter appropriate details for Bank Giro credit.

---

1 'Required' is defined 'Exactly as ordered'.
2 See page 32.

Time allowed: 15 mins

PRAXITELES GROUP

A fictitious organisation for examination purposes only

PRAXITELES HOUSE · ADAM STREET · LONDON WC2N 6EZ
TELEPHONE 01 930 5115

Our ref FENTY/BJ

Your ref

Darby & Co
PO Box 1690 B
Navigation House
Wellington Street
REDHILL RH44 6OK

Dear Sirs

MV HOPEAWAY — 17 cases

We confirm telephone conversation today cancelling our provisional booking for the above shipment. We understand our Ms Dankey has already contacted you for reallocation.

The consignee has informed us that 17 cases wl not be available for shipment until next month. As the Bill of Lading has not been prepared we trust you wl not be inconvenienced in this matter.

Yours ffly
PRAXITELES FREIGHT

Barry Jones
Shipping Clerk

Note: This is the **only** method that will satisfactorily separate word and figure *in the text*:

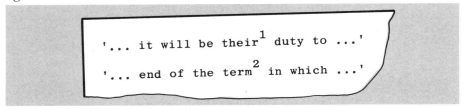

```
'... it will be their¹ duty to ...'

'... end of the term² in which ...'
```

b) Leave at least one space after the figure(s):

In the footnote   *In the text*

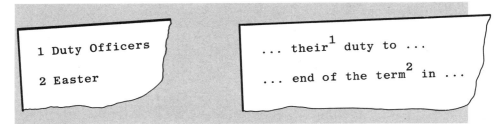

```
1 Duty Officers

2 Easter
```

```
... their¹ duty to ...

... end of the term² in ...
```

There is no penalty in the exam for the style you use to present footnotes so long as the aim of separating them is achieved.

If you wish, you may use both devices in the footnotes, that is, raise the figure *and* leave a space after it. (You *must* do both of these when you make the note in the text.)

- FOLLOW THE STYLE IN THE DRAFT – copy any separating line but don't add one.

- SEPARATE ITEMS for easy reading.

- BE CONSISTENT when presenting more than one footnote.

PRACTICE MATERIAL
Practise typing footnotes in the following tasks:

Time allowed:
Preparation   4 mins
Typing   10 mins
Checking/correcting   4 mins
                    ─────────
                    18 mins

Task 55

EMBROIDERY CATALOGUE

~~Items~~ Patterns in Stock

Item	Size	Colour Codes	
		UK*	USA
Picture	300 mm × 450 mm	ZAR16	B91
Cushion Cover	500 mm × 500 mm	ZAX2	E75a
Bedspread	1800 mm × 900 mm	YAX51	T83
Calendar	600 mm × 750 mm	KEY84	C100
Stool Cover	250 mm × 350 mm	DRM4	D24A

* Standard colours in Document T/189/ALBION

B5 · SPECIAL MARKS

URGENT   PERSONAL   PRIVATE AND CONFIDENTIAL
BY HAND   FOR THE ATTENTION OF THE SALES MANAGER

Special marks must be clearly seen, so they must be set apart from other items by at least one clear line space.

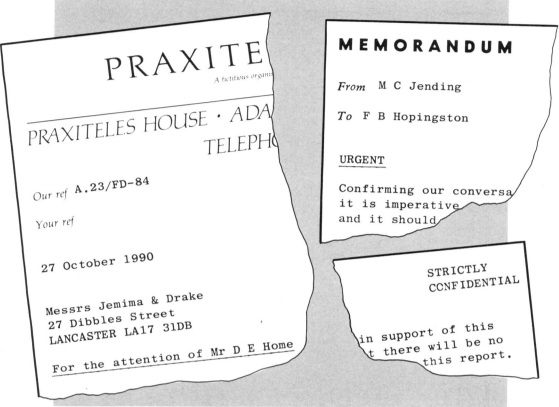

When a special mark is required in the exam (Part 1 only) this will be indicated. You will **not** be expected to infer that you should, for example, mark an item URGENT from wording that refers to a matter requiring urgent attention. Instead, the draft will specifically ask you to include a mark.

- LEAVE A CLEAR LINE space above and below special marks.

- TYPE the mark at the top of document and/or label but near enough to the address to be seen QUICKLY AND CLEARLY.

C9 SPACE BETWEEN ITEMS: FOOTNOTES

If the writer includes a line across the page to separate the footnote(s) from the text, you should of course include it and leave at least one clear line space above and below the line.

You should not add such a line if there is none in the draft: you cannot assume that the writer forgot it! Both styles – with and without a line – are commonly used.

In either case, the aim is to help the reader by making the footnote(s) easy to distinguish from the main text. The general rule applies for this purpose: **leave at least one clear line space before each footnote**.

Typing two footnotes

Two footnotes may occur in one task and will be identified by figures, e.g.

Figures and words must not run together. There are two ways in which to achieve this:

a) Raise the figure one-half line space:

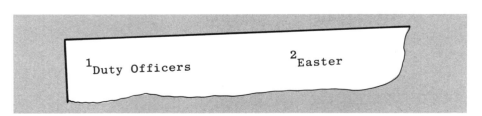

The following tasks will give you the opportunity to practise syllabus items B1 – B5:

Task 23

39 Acorn Way
Longfields
DERBY DE32 8XZ

The Manager
Rivelin Hotel
Bangley Drive
SCARBOROUGH
YO42 8HV

Dear Sir/Madam

I confirm telephone conversation today when I reserved accom for the nights of 22-29 September next.

A single room with bath is required, & I do not expect to arrive until approx 9 pm on 22 Sept.

Yrs ffly

Bernice H Jallow (Ms)

Task 24

39 Acorn Way
L——
D——

PERSONAL

Miss M Parry
Personnel Officer
P & W Benson Ltd
South Berry Street
SCARBOROUGH YO56 9HB

Dear Mary

Training Course: 23-30 Sept ——

Thank you for yr invitation to attend this course & to meet you on 22nd at 2 o'clock pm.

I have booked accom at
The Rivelin H——
(give address)

& told them I don't expect to arrive until around 9 o'clock pm. We should have time to visit Ahmed, & to see Mrs Patel if the opp occurs.

Best wishes,

Task 25

(Use a Praxiteles Group Letterhead)

The Crayford Company plc
Unit 6B
Bertway Industrial Park
LIVERPOOL   L34 8BY

Dear Sirs

Yr Order No 68214/x

Thank you for the above order. // Item 4 of your order refers to Staging Code TLP8 for use w our 'Colchester' Greenhouse. In fact, this Staging is not suitable for fitting in the 'Col——' which uses Staging from our FxA range.

We sh be glad if you wl confirm the size of yr Greenhouse so we can determine wch FxA Staging shd be supplied.

Yrs ffly
PRAXITELES BUILDINGS

Task 26

To Printing Supervisor
From A J Koper

(Memo)

Will you please review the contents of the literature featuring (related) Staging to the 'Col——' range of G'houses.

This request follows rec of several orders for Staging from the TLP range to fit 'Col——' units & I am wondering if our latest leaflets are in any way ambiguous in this respect.

Task 53

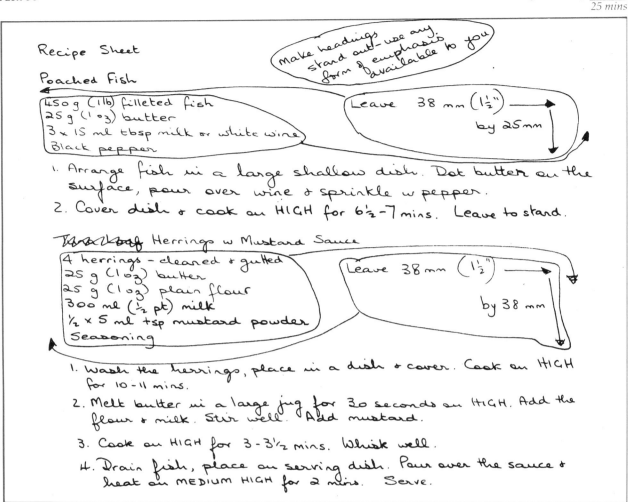

Recipe Sheet

Poached Fish

Make headings stand out - use any form of emphasis available to you

450 g (1lb) filleted fish
25 g (1 oz) butter
3 x 15 ml tbsp milk or white wine
Black pepper

Leave 38 mm (1½") by 25mm

1. Arrange fish in a large shallow dish. Dot butter on the surface, pour over wine & sprinkle w pepper.

2. Cover dish & cook on HIGH for 6½-7 mins. Leave to stand.

Herrings w Mustard Sauce

4 herrings - cleaned & gutted
25 g (1 oz) butter
25 g (1 oz) plain flour
300 ml (½ pt) milk
½ x 5 ml tsp mustard powder
Seasoning

Leave 38 mm (1½") by 38 mm

1. Wash the herrings, place in a dish & cover. Cook on HIGH for 10-11 mins.

2. Melt butter in a large jug for 30 seconds on HIGH. Add the flour & milk. Stir well. Add mustard.

3. Cook on HIGH for 3-3½ mins. Whisk well.

4. Drain fish, place on serving dish. Pour over the sauce & heat on MEDIUM HIGH for 2 mins. Serve.

Task 54

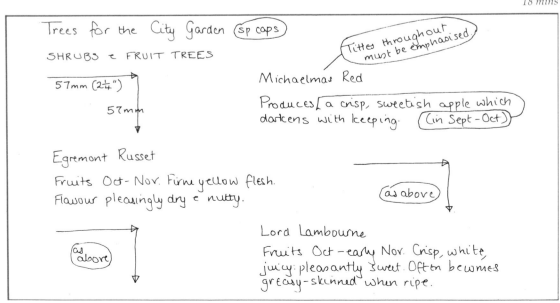

Trees for the City Garden (sp caps)

SHRUBS & FRUIT TREES

57mm (2¼")
57mm

Titles throughout must be emphasised

Michaelmas Red

Produces [a crisp, sweetish apple which darkens with keeping. (in Sept - Oct)

Egremont Russet

Fruits Oct - Nov. Firm yellow flesh.
Flavour pleasingly dry & nutty.

(as above)

Lord Lambourne

Fruits Oct - early Nov. Crisp, white, juicy, pleasantly sweet. Often becomes greasy-skinned when ripe.

(as above)

B6 ENCLOSURES

Reading

Enclosure marks are not written in RSA exam papers in Typewriting Skills. In Part 1 of Stage II you will be expected to show that an enclosure is referred to in one of the documents. The need for an enclosure mark will be implied by the wording, e.g.

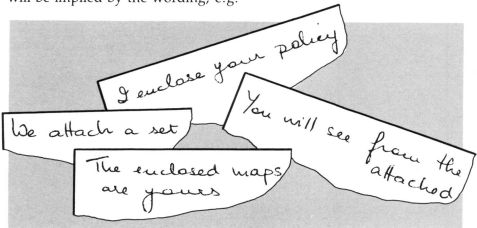

You may use any method of referring to an enclosure, either in the margin alongside the wording that mentions it, or at the foot of the document e.g.

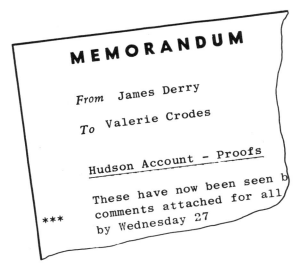

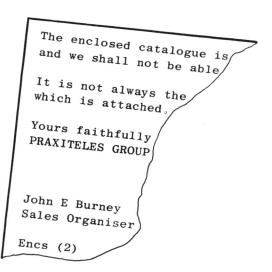

Using your machine to measure

It is not always possible to reserve an area by hand ruling before typing. You can use your machine to measure if you remember that on:

    10-pitch: 10 characters = 25 mm (1 in.) ⎤
    12–pitch: 12 characters = 25 mm (1 in.) ⎦ across the page
     6 typing lines = 25 mm (1 in.) down the page:

Method to leave horizontal space:
Start from point below 'W'.
In 10–pitch/12–pitch move across 21/25 spaces to right leaving 20/24 spaces clear. Type next part of copy.

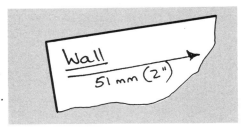

Method to leave vertical space:
Start from line on which 'Wall' is typed. Turn up 10 single-line spaces (to leave 9 line spaces (1½ in./38 mm) clear).
Type 'Ceiling'.

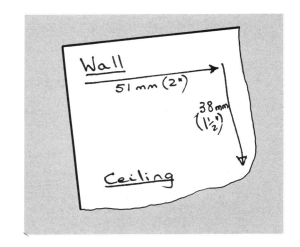

PRACTICE MATERIAL

Tasks 53 and 54 require you to:

a) give emphasis to certain items;
b) allocate space;
c) use consistently styles of presentation for abbreviations, headings, etc.

Practise setting-up and typing them in the times suggested. Check the above items in your work. Then ask someone else if they could suggest any improvements to the display you used.

- In the exam, ENCLOSURES will be implied in PART 1 ONLY.

- It will NOT ALWAYS be with the letter – so READ every task.

- No particular way of referring to an enclosure is required. The test is: WILL YOU NOTICE and REMEMBER?

PRACTICE MATERIAL
Take care to spot enclosures in the following tasks:

Task 27

Interim
Report on visit to Bakebury Products Ltd

The visit
~~This~~ followed a request from their A/cs Manager for assistance w their info flow. They ~~were~~ are experiencing bottlenecks at sales invoice points coupled w peaks in work. ~~at vari~~

We were able to spend ~~2~~ two half-days in their offices, on 21st and 28th of last month, observing e analysing the procedures as laid down and implemented. ~~The~~ Time was allocated to the departments/sections listed below, and ~~the attached set of notes out~~ an outline of the procedures ~~and flow chart~~ is included in the attached flow chart.

Sales Dept	Accounts Dept	Despatch Dept
Order section:	Invoicing	Delivery Notes
Telephone		Advice
Forms		Packing
Letters		Assembly

Reports on findings are currently being completed.

Task 28

Extract for inclusion in the Staff Bulletin ~~and~~ to be accompanied by the enclosed illustration, ~~and~~

"The work of the local artist, Mr H. Briscoe-Parke, is attracting attention from collectors all over the country. Mr Briscoe-Parke paints landscapes from ~~his~~ the area in which he was born and has lived for many years. Bridgnorth and its environs provide scenery and views which never fail to enchant him, as can be seen in this ~~illustration~~ example, 'Hilltop, Shropshire'."

C7 ALLOCATING SPACE

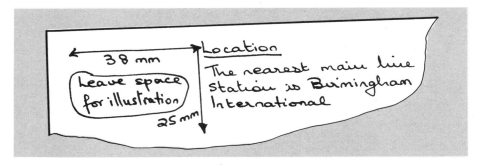

It may seem an easy matter to allocate space in accordance with instructions, but many typists incur exam penalties through leaving insufficient space at the places shown.

Measure and mark

The quickest and most reliable method is to mark your paper before you begin to type. If you mark lightly in pencil the areas to be left clear, you can then fit your typing around them as appropriate. In the exam, remember to remove the pencil marks before submitting your work.

Extra spaces

In drafts where arrows stop short of surrounding text, you may be unsure whether you should leave more space than the measurement given:

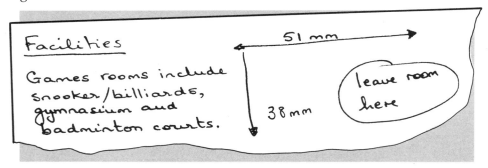

The general principle applies: **all words and other items must be separated by at least one clear space or line space.** If you are in any doubt because of the way in which the instruction is given, you will not be penalised for extra space.

Watch the arrows

In the example tasks above arrows mark the space to be measured:

a) right up to the surrounding text; *or*
b) stopping short of surrounding text (see previous paragraph 'Extra spaces').

It is important to make sure that you do not begin (or finish) typing within the area that should be left clear.

B7 LABELS

It is important to be able to use the typewriter parts, that is, the card holder, paper bail and grip rollers, to hold small stationery; and to type on varying thicknesses and qualities of paper.

In Part 1 of the exam you will be instructed to type **two** address labels. One of the addresses will be included in the text, not set out at the top of the document, e.g.

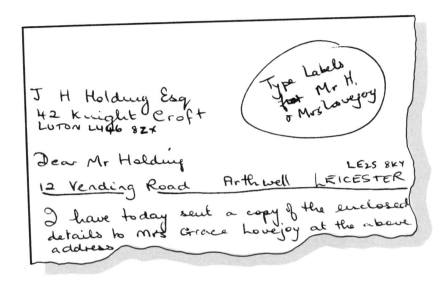

To be typed as:

Mrs G Lovejoy 12 Vending Road Arthwell LEICESTER LE25 8KY	J H Holding Esq 42 Knight Croft LUTON LU46 8ZX

N.B. Labels supplied in the exam are 7.5 cm (3") × 5 cm (2").

- TWO labels are to be addressed.
- Labels may not be for the same task. They may not always be for the letter.

Deciding what emphasis to use

In Part 2 of the exam the notice or draft advertisement that you will be asked to type will include instructions to emphasise certain items. No specific style of emphasis will be prescribed. For example:

> Give emphasis to words marked *
>
> May I remind you that our Summer Fayre* will be held on 14 July from 2 pm to 5.30 pm.

Only if you fail to add any emphasis at all to the items shown, will any penalty be incurred. You are therefore free to choose from the methods available to you. As well as those shown above, your machine may have emboldening and 'reverse type' functions. You may use these methods of emphasis in your exam work if they are available on your typewriter.

PRACTICE MATERIAL

Practise adding emphasis to items indicated in the following task:

Task 52

Time allowed:
Planning	5 mins
Typing	10 mins
Checking	5 mins
	20 mins

> Type the following in the form of a notice for display in a waiting room. Separate or paragraph the wording and give emphasis to the words underlined. Time yourself from reading this to completion of accurate copy.

Weight Reducing Diet — This diet shd be undertaken only on the advice of + under the supervision of a Doctor. The instructions are easy to carry out but must be observed without any modifications or lapses; it is useless partly to obey them. When your weight is down to normal you can return to your ordinary diet but check any tendency to regain weight by restricting consumption of articles in Instruction A. Instructions. 1. EAT as much as you like of Lean Meat, Poultry, Game, Rabbit, Hare, Liver, Kidney, Heart + Sweetbread — cooked in any way but without using flour, breadcrumbs or thick sauces. Fish, boiled or steamed only. Potatoes boiled, steamed or baked in skins. Other vegetables of all kinds. 2 You may have milk (not condensed) up to half a pint daily. No cream. 3 You may have 3 small slices of bread per day. 4 You may have nothing else whatever Particularly note this means no butter, margarine, fat or oils, sugar, jam, sweets, chocolate or puddings.

B8 UNFAMILIAR AND/OR FOREIGN WORDS

Foreign words are not deliberately included in every exam, but words such as 'cafe' and 'restaurant', which are foreign in origin, may appear in any of the tasks.

When words occur that are likely to be unfamiliar to most people, they are written clearly so that you may **copy** them accurately. Names are an important example. The context and meaning of sentences should help you to decipher other types of word, but this method does not work for names.

When you come across a word you do not recognise, or cannot read:

- try to find similar word(s) elsewhere in the task;
- read the whole sentence, and if necessary surrounding sentences, to see if the sense, or meaning, will help identify the difficult word;
- write down the letters you think are in the word;
- once you finally decide what the letters must be, if these make a word you still do not recognise, look in your dictionary to check if the word exists before you type it;
- if all else fails, it sometimes helps to stop thinking about the word for a moment or two. For instance, you could read through and start planning another task. After a short diversion it may be easier to decipher the problem word.

> - COPY foreign or unfamiliar words, names and addresses.
>
> - HAVE PATIENCE to check them letter by letter.
>
> - USE YOUR DICTIONARY. Don't type odd words in sentences unless you're sure the words exist. If a sentence doesn't make sense to you even after you've checked meanings, it is likely to be wrong.

Fictitious details

Names of products, companies or individuals and addresses, etc., used in exam drafts are fictitious. In order to make them more realistic, proper town names are often used; but beyond the town all other details may be false.

Task 51

Time allowed:
Preparation 5 mins
Typing 15 mins
Checking/correcting 5 mins
25 mins

STATISTICS TABLE NO 272

Value Rating Categories	Density in Growth		Percentage of European VRs
	UK #%	England only #%	
Value Ratings			
1.6	42	19	8
8.7	22	8	66
16.0	16	16	22
24.0	28	33	91
31.6	54	12	43
68.2	17	11	23
92.4	15	13	38
Ratios			
A	22	27	29
B	16	14	29.7
C	12	10	84
Variables			
S, D	12	10	84
F, G	14	19	82
T, X	92	47	28
E, M	87	73	42

The above figures do not represent up-to-date indexes and cannot be relied upon to determine statistical values other than those outlined in Table 221.

C4   GIVING EMPHASIS

Major items in business documents, as well as notices, etc., often require emphasis to attract attention. Typewriting methods of giving emphasis include:

- capitals
- spaced capitals
- initial capitals with underlining
- insetting

PLEASE NOTE:-

J U M B L E   S A L E

Will Be Held Next Week!

Everyone is welcome.
We need as much help
as we can get!!

If the name of your own town, or any town with which you are familiar, appears in exam tasks you may know that streets, districts, counties or postcodes are non-existent or incorrect.

In the real business world companies as well as individuals may consider it discourteous if their name is typed incorrectly, while the importance of copying addresses accurately is obvious.

In a case of doubt in the office you would be able to check with someone else before making any changes; in the exam you must rely on what is clearly before you. It is not necessary for you to detect errors in facts in drafts. Do not confuse this with circled words which contain errors for you to correct (see syllabus item B9).

B9 CORRECTING MATERIAL CONTAINING ERRORS

We shall be glad if you will no**w** let us have a**n** copy of the document which has been received ~~fro~~ Mr Marshall at your address.

In the above draft, the writer has amended the text to show the typist what to type, that is, how to correct the work.

In the draft below the writer has merely indicated which words are wrong and is relying on the typist to decide how to correct the work:

It is (no) always (possibel) to check documents (fro) day to day (becuase) (there) (sauce) is not known

Reading for sense

From the above example you will see that you often need to check the meaning of the full sentence to make sure what the correction should be. 'Fro' may require correcting to 'for' or 'from'.

Errors of agreement

Two girls used to (walks) down the street each morning on (her) way to work.
Tomorrow they will (talked) about the matter.

In this example the errors are of the same kind: the words in each

ITEMS FOR COMPLETION & TIME SCHEDULE

Item	Requirement		Days' Work
	Draft	Completed*	
General Syllabus Guidelines Spec. Paper	October November December	December January March	3½ 1 2½
Books Book 2 Core Skills Stage 3	September January August	March July February	14 36 48
Armed Forces Air Force Royal Marines Army Training Royal Navy	October October October October	October October Oct — Oct —	1 3 1½ 0½

* For Approval

Time allowed:
Reading/noting   *1 min*
Typing/ruling   *15 mins*
Checking/correcting   *5 mins*
                     20 mins

sentence do not 'match' each other. The sentences should be corrected to 'Two girls used to walk down the street each morning on their way to work' and 'Tomorrow they will talk about the matter'.

Punctuation errors

Punctuation errors, including mistakes in the use of apostrophes, will also be circled for you to correct.

> There will be, however, much speculation about the causes of Mr Smiths problem. We shall of course not, be able to help you. if you do not tell us more; details about this matter. We cannot be expected to dispel rumour without your help.

To be typed as:

```
There will be, however, much speculation about the causes
of Mr Smith's problem.  We shall of course not be able to
help you if you do not tell us more details about this
matter.  We cannot be expected to dispel rumour without
your help.
```

Spelling

Some of the words circled will be mis-spellings, e.g.

> We can rely on you to take the neccesary steps untill further more permenant arrangments are made.

As in the above example, the misspelt words will be words in common use which can easily be checked in a dictionary.
(See also syllabus item B4(a) on page 5.)

Practise setting up quickly for typing in columns. For the following tasks, drill until you can:

a) insert paper;
b) set margins;   } in less than two minutes.
c) set tabulator stops

Task 49

Extract - Balance Sheet at 31 March 1990

(capitals)

	1985 £	1986 £
Fixed Assets		
Housing:	16,040,195	27,050,196
Offices:	3,412,380	3,269,186
	19,452,575	30,319,382
Less:		
Equity: £217,642		£247,642
Grant: 1,003,830		—
	1,221,472	247,642
	£18,231,103	£30,071,740

	£	
Current Assets		
Sundry Debtors:	£224,149	HS 115,226
Cash:	62,122	26,331
	286,271	141,593
Less:		
Sundry Creditors:	£2³89,918	122,966
Overdrafts:	60,280	256,866
	300,198	379,832
	(£13,927)	(£238,239)

Remember: Leave at least one space between longest column-items and the first figure (or character) in next column)
Use your interliner to rule double lines under totals

Type the following tasks, correcting all errors:

Task 29

Mr J Hanworth
% Messrs Kenwood + Co
Ferrypoint House
Barlingham Road
DERBY   DE28 42BT

Type on a letterhead

Dear Jim

Sorry to have to write to ~~address~~ you at your office but have mislaid your new home address details, & apparently you are not yet on the phone.

The Club Ctee ~~Committee~~ Meeting has been brought forward to Monday 6 Nov at 7 pm, (Agenda attached) and ~~as we~~ after our discussions last month I know you'll want to be there if at all possible. Peter had failed to record your change of address so Heather has sent your official notice of the change to Challen Road. ~~but~~ Whilst it may get forwarded in time I thought it was worth this note to make sure you don't miss the opp to make your very urgent points on the matter of the new subscription rates.

Yours sincerely

Task 30

~~May~~ We invite you to our Reception at the Grand hotel
on Mondy 31 january next, at 5 pm.

The occasion is the 75th Aniversary of the opening of
our Sheffield Branch.

We look forward to meeting you and hope you will bring
a guest.

The syllabus allows you to type material in columns in:

blocked style, e.g.   **indented style**, e.g.

centred style, e.g.

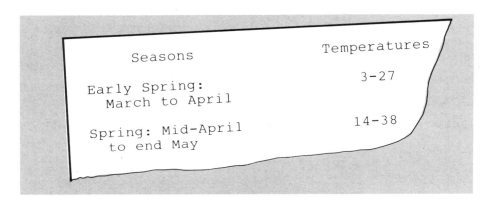

Columns of figures may be blocked, but, if they are to be totalled, figures should be ranged to the right:

1
11
111
1111

You will not be penalised for inconsistency if you range a column of figures to the right in a task where you are using block style for columns of words. Columns of figures are not the same type of item and there are overriding reasons for presenting them in this way.

Leave space for ruling.

> ■ When typing material in columns as the basis for a ruled table (see item B12 on page 74) all you need do is to leave space for the ruling, which you can then insert by hand after completing typing.

We (do,) not believe that
our products can be beaten
for (q ality),. and (price) is
also a major consideration,
and we are confident that
our company is now able
to (compeet) with any
other manufacturer.

Automation (have) brought(s)
many benefits (by) including
improvement in reliability.

How are we to know if our (goosd) are not
(unsatisfactoly) if dissatisfied (customer):
do not contact (ux)?

It is no good writing to the local
(newpaper) or complaining to the BBC if we
have not first had an (oportunity) of (putti)
putting the matter (wright.)

(Bbbody) knows the trouble (were) in if
nobody tells us the truth.

B10   ROUTING CARBON COPIES

In the exam you will be asked to take two carbon copies of one document.

The extra copy

The destination of the extra copy will be referred to in the draft but not set out separately for you to copy. You must read the draft to find the detail(s).

All copies

Routing details should appear on the top copy and both carbon copies, unless you are explicitly told otherwise. It will save time if you type the details at the bottom of the document while you still have the complete 'pack' together in the machine.

You may use any style of presentation, e.g.

cc Miss Atkinson
Copy to Miss Atkinson
CC: Miss Atkinson
Copy: Miss Atkinson

Practise inserting leader dots in the following task:

Task 48

FORTIFIED WINES

Type, rule + check your own work. Then ask someone else to check or comment on it

SHERRY

Fino and Manzanilla

ref	* bottled in Spain	bottle	dozen
5429	Fino, with nutty dry flavour	£3.45	£40.20
6494	+ Manzanilla . - - - - - - - .	3.80	44.40
6413	* Fino San Patricio. - - - - - - -	4.00	46.80
6500	Fino Inocente . - - - - - - - .	4.75	55.80

PORT

ref	* bottled at source	bottle	dozen
6037	Old Tawny . - - - - - - - -	9.40	111.60
6046	*Warre's Nimrod — - - . .	7.95	94.20
6301	Martinez Tawny	12.00	142.80

CASE No 8607 at £25
one bottle each of
Fino, Manzanilla,
Fino Inocente
Old Tawny, Martinez Tawny
Warre's Nimrod

Leave 51 mm (2") from left margin

Material in columns

Every exam will include a table with three columns for ruling (see
syllabus item A8). One of the columns will be subdivided, and some of
the column headings will take more than one line. For example:

MEDIA TABLE XI

Programmes	Availability	Costs for Items 21 and 22	
		£	$
Radio BBC Independent	National Regional	9m 3m	7m 2.3 m
Television BBC 1 2			

Type the following task:

Task 33

Memo

From J Deeming   To Fred Jarrington

You asked me last week to let you have the figures for home and overseas sales of goods in Category 4. You wl remember I was unable to give you a straightforward answer until I had collected some of the data from Joe Maxton.

This was because Category 4 items may be sold direct via main agents or thro' distributors & there is the added complication that some overseas orders are (credited) to UK agents.

However, after I have now compiled the following data and I hope it will serve your purpose.

SALES OF CAT 4 GOODS (£000's)

HOME

1985	1986	1987 to date	Item No
	18	11	C 2409
	9	5	B 8216

OVERSEAS

Direct

1986	1987	Indirect (via UK Agents) 1986	1987	Item No
22	18	9	2	C 2409
31	22	4	2	B 8216

Time allowed:
Reading   3 mins
Typing   13 mins
Checking   4 mins
                 20 mins

C3 CONSISTENCY

Leader dots

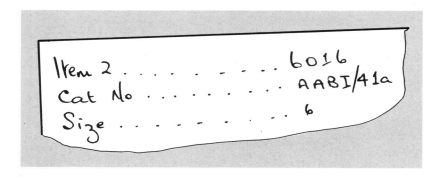

A row of continuous dots serves to lead the eye from one column to another.

Alternatively, you may like to add the refinement of grouping dots and spaces, e.g.

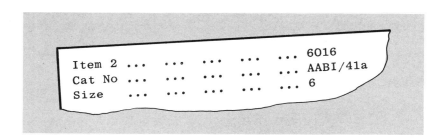

The RSA syllabus allows you to use any grouping, but you must be consistent in whatever style you choose.

Accuracy faults: the word prior to the start of your leader dots must have a space after it (see marking scheme B(c)).

As well as normal words, a series of characters (including spaces) making a recognisable unit, such as a line of leader dots, is defined as a word in the marking scheme. Therefore, a clear space must also be left after the end of your leader dots, as after an ordinary word.

TIMED EXAM PRACTICE FOR PART 1

Below are three typical Part 1 exam tasks with target completion times. The tasks will help you to check your rate of production, accuracy and presentation.

When you have completed them fill in the personal progress record for Part 1 – in the stationery section at the back of this book – to help you monitor your progress.

Time allowed:
Reading	*3 mins*
Typing	*10 mins*
Checking	*3 mins*
	16 mins

Task 34

NOTICE

Take 2 carbon copies

It has been our custom to arrange an annual one-day seminar for our f/t & p/t Instructors. This yr we are extending this to a two-day meeting on a Friday & Sat in November. We cannot offer accom but there are a number of good hotels in the area.

Our topic for this venture is The Electronic Office & we hope to assemble an exhibition w demonstrations of the latest equipment. Leading experts in this field with conduct working sessions, as well as leading discussion groups.

You may wish to take the opp to benefit from our programme (copy of which is attached) & we sh be delighted if you can join us. // You wl appreciate th numbers are limited, so please return the enclosed form duly completed asap, so that a place can be reserved for you. There is a charge of £3 for lunch & refreshments each day (total £6). but lunch can be arranged

We look forward to meeting you or welcoming you back if you have previously attended our annual seminars.

If you wish to make separate luncheon arrangements please make note on the form as requested.

---

ii) **check** you have made a pencil note in the draft of any extra clear line spaces you intend to incorporate (if your count is more than twenty-nine because you intend to leave more than the minimum of one clear line space between items, e.g. after headings).

iii) **recall** the number of typewriting line spaces in sizes of paper:

A4 = 70
A5 = 35
A5 (shorter edge at top) = 50

iv) **check** which size(s) will be large enough. You will see that A5 (longer edge at top) paper will be too short.

v) **check** which size will be more appropriate for the purpose (will A5 attract sufficient attention to, say, a notice?).

Repeat the **count/check/recall/check** routine for the width:

i) **count** the spaces required across the page for the draft. For example, in the draft used above there are thirty-four characters/spaces.

ii) **check** you have made a note in the draft of any extra spaces (for example, before and after vertical lines) that you intend to incorporate (if your count is more than thirty–four because you intend to leave more than the minimum of one clear space after the longest item in each column).

iii) **recall** the number of typewriter character spaces across sizes of paper:
12-pitch: A4 = 100; A5 = 100; A5 (shorter edge at top) = 70
10-pitch: A4 = 82; A5 = 82; A5 (shorter edge at top) = 60

iv) **check** which size(s) will be large enough. You will see there would be enough space for margins (say, 25 mm/1 in.) on A4 or A5.

v) **check** your line space count, as above, and the decisions you made then.

There is no penalty in the exam for the decision you make about the use of A4 or A5 plain paper. It is important to check that your work will fit the paper you choose, because you **will** receive penalties if the paper is too small, causing any of the following faults:

- *overtyping effect* i.e. insufficient space for ruling, which means lines cross typing (Accuracy fault)
- *no horizontal space after words and lines* (Accuracy fault)
- *no clear line space separating different items* e.g. ruling and typing (presentation fault – see marking scheme C9)
- *sloping lines* caused by being too close to the bottom of paper, i.e. inconsistent line spacing (presentation fault).

- A4 IS SAFEST for medium-length and long work.

- Use the COUNT/CHECK/RECALL/CHECK routine to decide size for SHORT work.

Memo

From AJP

To Mary Kendalton
        Reprographics Department

[The Notice refers to the programme being attached. You will remember we discussed this. The Notice sent to the printers is in fact the second one wh you wl produce. The first 500 wl have this ref deleted. I hope you remember this & that it is clear what is required.

Annual Seminar

I enclose copy of the notice in respect of the above. You wl remember I mentioned this last week. Copy of the notice has been sent to the company who are printing the broc offical programs for their info but they are aware you wl be producing the first Notice for inclusion in a mail-shot. // I wd suggest an run-off initially of 500 & after checking the paper you suggested, I agree the yellow sheet is the most appropriate. // Can you let me have a proof copy before the first is completed? job I'm sure you wl make a special effort on the time, but we always seem to be rushing you.

Time allowed:
Reading   3 mins
Typing   10 mins
Checking   3 mins
                16 mins

Consideration of the shape of typed material is a refinement that distinguishes the excellent typist who can bring a professional quality to the work of an office as well as the essential qualities of accuracy and reasonable rate of production.

B) AMOUNT OF TEXT

Material	Destination*		Print No
	Home	Over-seas	
Duplette	997	1063	X1432
Marxit	648	294	Y4000

*The majority of items are dispersed

Here is a simple routine to avoid choosing stationery that is too short or too narrow.

To check for length:

i) **count** the lines in the draft table to be typed. For example, in the following draft there is a minimum of twenty-nine.

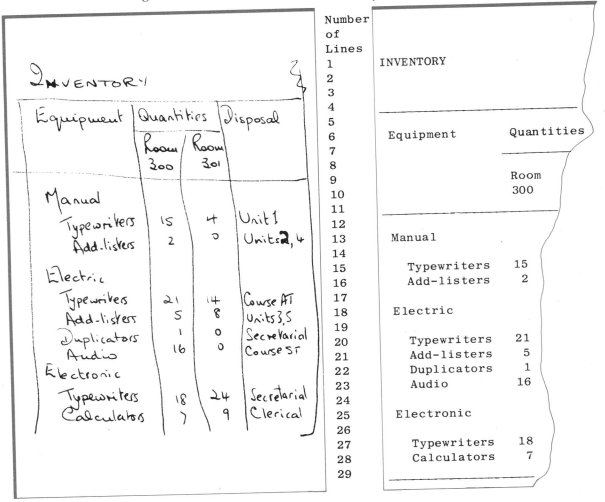

Our ref   AJP/Sem8

Your ref   Quot.14/87

Use letterhead to retype this letter into correction (circled handwritten note)

Messrs B T Gassman & Bros
5709 Grammington Road
DARLINGTON
Co Durham   DL33 8BZ

Dear (Sir)

Thank you for your quotation, reference as above, and we are pleased to place our order with you accordingly for printing of the brochures for our 2-day (seminor) in November. *Our official order is now will be forwarded direct from our order Section.*

The draft which we sent with our enquiry needs to be (amendmented) as follows:

1. The seminar will be held on a Friday and Saturday

2. Price of lunches is now *for the 2 days* (you have the draft Notice for them)

In addition, we now have the wording for paragraph 7 on the sixth fold of the mock-up:

"The typical instructor tends to be pleased when trainees enter the room, start the warm-up (activity) and proceed to type for 10 minutes or more. The (instructor) often uses this time for completing various administratrative duties such as takin register or counselling students absent from previous sessions. Completing these activities during the warm-up period is fine; however, the warm-up period often extends (afr) beyond an acceptable time period. These lengthy warm-ups are of little benefit) - three minutes are (suficient). The main objective of the (warmpup) (are) simply to "loosen up" the arms and fingers and to become reoriented to the machine. Longer times than three minutes (five at maximum) are simply a waste and tend to be boring. It is also likely that trainees will take time out for idle conversation (they will still have time for a warm-up!). When they know three minutes is the maximum they quickly begin work and any wasted time is kept to a minimum."

As arranged by telephone, we attach copy of the Notice being produced in our Rep Department.
We shall be glad if you will arrange for your representative to call, as promise in your earlier letter. The main item for discussion is the problem of (colours). As you pointed out in your letter, the combinations available are very different from those we have envisaged and our preference is governed by avoiding conflict with other publications *which* our organisation (issued) *providing with* we can find a way to achieve a distinct identity for this seminar as part of our general activities for instructors. We can be flexible in using the colours you advise, *providing* *maintain* *instructors.* *Programme*

give dates
The week after next, Tuesday or Thursday, would be convenient for us, or the Friday morning. only. We shall be glad, however, if An appointment shd be made through Mr Jim Davis on extension 281, secretary to Administration Officer.

Yours faithfully
PRAXITELES GROUP

A J Prentiss
Seminar Programme Director

JUMBLE SALE

Can you help by bringing your own or collecting your
friends' and neighbours' jumble?

We need clothing, crockery, old books, records and
tapes in particular.   Any household items are also
welcome.

We also need help to transport donated goods to the
Village Hall by Friday of next week.

If you can help, phone Marjorie Wilks

on 9986-420149

JUMBLE SALE

Can you help by
bringing your own
or collecting your
friends' and
neighbours' jumble?

We need clothing,
crockery, old books,
records and tapes in
particular.   Any
household items are
also welcome.

We also need help to
transport donated goods
to the Village Hall by
Friday of next week.

If you can help,
phone Marjorie Wilks

on 9986-420149

Communication: the use of the same spacing around similar items in different parts of a document can help the reader to see and compare related information. For example,

---

PERFECT PRINTS WITH PRAXIFOTO

PRINTING

The versatile new multi-format masking

frame allows economical use of paper.

PHONE US ON 882-4396531 for your free

copy of latest manuals and price list.

CREATIVITY

The new units offer attractive and

creative opportunities for new work.

Our prices are competitive. If you

find the same item for less elsewhere

we will refund the difference.

PERFECT PRINTS WITH PRAXIFOTO

PRINTING

The versatile new multi-format masking
frame allows economical use of paper.

PHONE US ON 882-4396531 for your free

copy of latest manuals and price list.

CREATIVITY

The new units offer attractive and
creative opportunities for new work.

Our prices are competitive. If you

find the same item for less elsewhere

we will refund the difference.

There are some general requirements for presentation of all your work in both parts of the exam. These are concerned with:

- stationery (see also Section Four);
- clean and uncreased work;
- blocked or centred styles;
- margins;
- space between items;
- corrections.

These are discussed in Chapter 7, that is, syllabus items C1, C2, C5, C8, C9 and C10, pages 16–24.

C3   CONSISTENCY

When drafting documents for typing, writers are often in a hurry and rely on the typist to alter inconsistencies which may distract the reader.

Obvious changes in style may affect speed and ease of reading, and should be avoided. For example 'The train leaves at 2pm and arrives at 1500 hrs' may cause hesitation, and 'We took only 4 pounds but there were 6 lb of strawberries ready' could be misleading.

a) Abbreviations, b) words or figures, c) words or symbols

The inconsistencies to be included in the exam will be selected from:

a) **abbreviations** for measurements (e.g. cm   mm   ft   ins   6'   6")
weights (e.g. k   kg   lb   oz)
time (e.g. pm   o'clock   hrs)
money (e.g. p/pence,   BF,   DM)
b) **words or figures** (quantities only)
c) **words or symbols** (e.g $ £   %   dash/hyphen key indicating 'to')

In Part 1 of the exam some of the above will be written in different styles for you to 'spot' them and to present them in consistent style.

The test is whether or not you will notice them, and present both examples of the same type of item in the same way.

You may choose the style and will not be penalised, so long as you are consistent.

GENERAL REQUIREMENTS

There are some general requirements for presentation of all your work in both parts of the exam. These are concerned with:

- stationery (see also below);
- clean and uncreased work;
- blocked or centred styles;
- margins;
- space between items;
- corrections;

These are discussed in Chapter 7, that is syllabus items C1, C2, C5, C8, C9 and C10, pages 16–24.

> ■ REMEMBER, the general requirements on presentation apply throughout the exam. PRACTISE them in all typewriting tasks.
>
> ■ DON'T BE CONTENT WITH SHODDY WORK.

C1 STATIONERY

Apart from the obvious need to use the printed form to enter appropriate details, you will not be given instructions on the type or size of stationery to use.

Deciding which size stationery to use

Two major factors in making your decision must be:

a) the purpose of the document;
b) the amount of text.

A) PURPOSE

The impact of a notice, draft advertisement or ruled table will be lost if the reader has to turn to a second page. In any of these items blank space(s), that is, extra clear line spaces or wider spaces between columns, can be used to good effect. Such extra clear space serves two purposes: to shape your work to fit the paper and to aid communication.

Shape: wider margins and extra line spaces left clear make work 'tall and thin'; for 'short and fat' you need narrow margins and minimum clear line spaces (if you are aiming for this shape, remember the syllabus requirements for a minimum of 13 mm (½ in.) margins at top and left, and at least one clear line space between separate items within a document).

PRACTICE MATERIAL

Copy Tasks 37 to 39, concentrating on using the same style to present the same type of abbreviations, etc. Remember, *you* choose the style.

Task 37

The patio ~~requires~~ ~~covers~~ measures approx 9 ft x 8' and the materials ordered include.

4 tons Builders' Sand
3 ton Gravel
10 x 1800 mm Ranch fence boards.

These items wl be delivered between 2 pm and 1600 hrs on Tuesday. The driver has been asked to collect payment at time of delivery (ie £56 plus five pounds delivery charge).

Task 38

"Type each line 3 times" has been a standard direction for many years, but ~~type~~ this typing the same thing three times does not extend skill. It is far superior to type from a wide variety of sources, typing as much as possible, ~~from~~ not only and not 100% from a textbook. At least 60 per cent of typing should be from own notes (for school or college work), magazines, newspapers, letters, handwritten work prepared by tutors.

Task 39

Write-Right

A pen with a 90-day money back satisfaction gtee.
                   are celebrities
Who ~~is~~ the ~~celebrity~~ who will be autographing ~~free~~ diaries for Write-Right purchasers?
Find out at DEGRIE'S DEPARTMENTAL STORE on TUESDAY.
    0930 — 10 am   Celebrity 1 — Film Star
    11—12 noon   Celebrity 2 — Star of Stage & Screen
    2 — 3 pm   Celebrity 3 — Pop Star

VERTICAL LINES

Some electronic typewriters are fitted with daisy wheels (instead of bar keys or golf-balls) which include a special character for vertical ruling. This can be used on each line so as to build up a continuous line dividing columns as required.

Without this facility, vertical ruling by typewriter involves removing the paper from the machine after completing the horizontal work. The paper is then re-inserted sideways so that the underline key can be used to complete the ruling. Considerable care is needed to align this ruling with the ends of the typed horizontal lines, particularly at corners.

GENERAL POINTS

Make sure that you use the underline key, as the dash/hyphen key does not type a continuous line.

On many typewriters there is danger of the ruling cutting through paper, because the pressure used to make the impression is concentrated on the small area of the underline character (you may have noticed the same effect with full stops and other small characters). Watch out for this, and if necessary consult your machine manual for guidance on how to reduce the pressure, sometimes called the 'touch' on manual machines, while you complete rulings.

Mixture of typewriter and hand ruling

Some people prefer to type rulings across the page (horizontal), to remove the work from the machine after completion of the horizontal work, and to rule lines down the page by hand. This is more practicable in the work situation than re-inserting the work sideways to type the vertical rulings, with all the careful adjustments needed to 'square-up' corners and make neat borders.

If you choose this method you will want to make sure your pen is the same colour as your typewriter ribbon to ensure a more professional appearance than the use of different colours in your ruling.

> ■ HAND RULING round material typed in columns is quick and easy.
>
> ■ MATERIALS are important for draft and final ruling.
>
> ■ CHECK PRESSURE if ruling by machine.

Errors in ruling

Each line in ruling is defined as one word (see marking scheme B(b) on page 9). Ruling errors are therefore penalised as:

Accuracy faults
- *any single line omitted* (see marking scheme B2.1)
- *no space between words/figures and vertical ruling* (see marking scheme B(c))
- *overtyping effect* e.g. ruling through words/figures (see marking scheme B1.5)

Presentation faults
- *failure to leave at least one clear line space between ruling and words/figures* (see marking scheme C9(e))

d) PUNCTUATION

You should use the same pattern of spaces after punctuation marks as they occur. You may leave the minimum requirement of one space every time; or you may choose to insert a different number of spaces after different types of punctuation, e.g. one space after each comma but two/three spaces after each full stop e.g.

Open or full punctuation:

Full punctuation   Open punctuation

```
24 February, 1990

Mr. F. T. A. Harding,
27, Churchwell Street,
Fairding Green, .
BOURNEMOUTH,
BH72 19BX.


Dear Sir,


P.A. Systems


Our catalogue is enclosed, but
we are not sure it is the one
required.


Please let us know.


Yours faithfully,


Enc.
```

```
24 February 1990

Mr F T A Harding
27 Churchwell Street
Fairding Green
BOURNEMOUTH
BH72 19BX


Dear Sir


PA Systems


Our catalogue is enclosed, but
we are not sure it is the one
required.


Please let us know.


Yours faithfully


Enc
```

In 'open' punctuation:

> all commas and full stops are omitted from addresses and other places where they are not grammatically necessary (they are necessary in sentences).

Most typists are now taught open-style punctuation, and find no difficulty in using it consistently. However, you should be careful when using this style to apply it to *all* items (e.g. 'PA' in the above example); otherwise you will receive a presentation fault for inconsistency.

draft can be typed in columns as shown below, ready for hand ruling after removal from the machine.

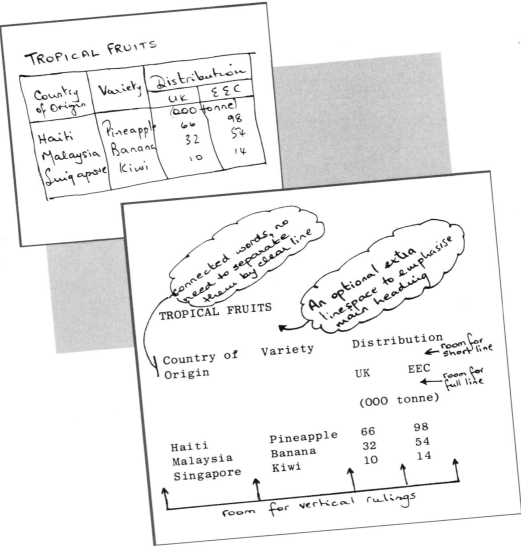

Typewriter ruling

This makes the typing of tables slightly more complicated.

HORIZONTAL LINES

You may choose to complete your typing of the material in columns (as suggested above for ruling by hand), before returning to appropriate points to type the lines. However, because the paper is still in the machine, you do not have the advantage of being able to see the length and position of your typing below the level at which you are ruling. Nor is there the opportunity to draft in pencil before final ruling.

If you wish to incorporate ruling with your typing of the table, it is necessary to count carefully the characters and spaces that will appear within and between the columns so that you know the length of rule required. When you have completed the top line, set tab stops at the first and last points of the rule. This makes it easier to rule subsequent lines: use the underliner at each of these tab stops before underlining to join the two. (For lines lower in the table this is more reliable than 'copying from a distance', and quicker than rolling the paper back to check where lines should end.)

e) Paragraphing

Blocked **or** indented paragraphs are acceptable. Only if you mix your styles within one task will there be penalty.

Special features of this scheme:

It is designed to meet individual requirements.

Assessment can take place at any time.

It leads to a recognised certificate plus possibility of endorsement.

James Johnson attended a secondary school in the Midlands and knows he is likely to need to know how to use a computer.

Mary Boniface is 19 years old and works in an office. If she can use a computer she is more likely to gain promotion.

Keith Wentworth works as a word processor operator in the offices at the steelworks.

Headed/numbered/lettered paragraphs or listed items will be included in Part 1 of the exam. Follow the layout used in the draft.

Remember, no particular style is required by the syllabus, so **make up your mind** what spacing you are going to use and stick to it throughout the task.

HOW TO HIRE

1.   Select the item required from the Catalogue.

2.   Complete Form D with catalogue details.

3.   Hand Form D, deposit and proof of identity to clerk.

Materials

(a) We shall order panels and roofing materials from London.

(b) Frames and Windows will be supplied locally.

CONSTRUCTION

(i)   Front - roll-up door

(ii)   Sides - removable with windows and doors

(iii)   Back - internal and external fixing

HOW TO HIRE

1   Select the item required from the Catalogue.

2   Complete Form D with catalogue details.

3   Hand Form D, deposit and proof of identity to clerk.

Materials

(a)   We shall order panels and roofing materials from London.

(b)   Frames and Windows will be supplied locally.

CONSTRUCTION

(i)   Front - roll-up door

(ii)   Sides - removable with windows and doors

(iii) Back - internal and external fixing

B12   RULING BY HAND AND/OR ON THE TYPEWRITER

You will not be required to rule in any task other than the Table (see syllabus item A6 on page 7) in the Stage II Typewriting Skills exam.
  The syllabus allows you to:

- rule all lines by hand; *or*
- rule all lines using the typewriter; *or*
- use a mixture of lines ruled using the typewriter and by hand (e.g. to type lines across the page and to rule by hand the vertical lines).

Ruling by hand

1   Use a flat, clean **ruler**. It should preferably be made of perspex with metric measurements.

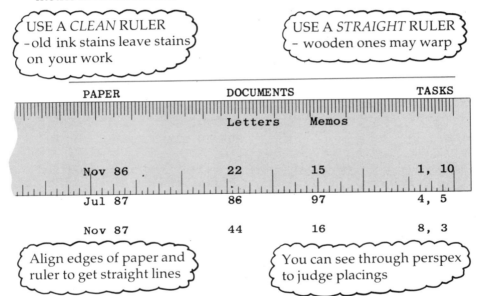

2   Experiment with **pens** (any type) until you find one that:

   a) produces fine (not thick) lines;
   b) does not blot (some ballpoints leave sticky blobs where you start and stop ruling).

3   Obtain a **pencil** (needs to have a soft lead e.g. 2B and a fine point):

   a) you can then rule first in pencil to ensure all your lines are straight and in the right place, before ruling in **pen**;
   b) if accurate pencil rulings are light and fine you can rule over them (without having to erase).

4   Always have a **soft eraser** with you for erasing pencil marks. (It will also be useful in Part 1 of the exam if you need to remove excess carbon before correcting carbon copies.)

  Ruling all lines by hand is the easiest method. All you need do is to type the material in columns, leaving extra space where lines are needed, so that you can rule them in without difficulty or any risk of ruling over your typing (overtyping effect). For example, the following hand written

PRACTICE MATERIAL

Practise typing lettered/numbered items consistently. Set margin and tab stops to help you move quickly and accurately to the different starting points in paragraphs and sub-paragraphs.

Task 40

3. Consequently the Committee has decided th the following general principles wl be taken into a/c in the management of the contraction anticipated in the relevant sector.

   3.1 As soon as numbers permit, those schools taking extra forms of entry shd revert to the number originally designated.

   3.2 Consideration shd also be given to a further reduction in the size of a form of entry.

Task 41

    2 EXTERNAL WORKS

Item 2.1 Front Garden

a Rake out joints of brickwork.

b Take up paving in front porch.

c Supply & lay quarry tile paving.

    2.2 Rear Garden

a Take down three stone steps.

b Take down timber step.

c Remove stone step from boiler room.

Task 42

(i) Today's official minimum for new dwellings is 4 inches of loft insulation, but six inches looks a better investment.

(ii) How do we arrive at 6 inches? A standard method is to add the cost of installation to the likely cost of heat loss.

(iii) Most joists are 4 in timber, so if yr insulation does not come to the top of them it needs topping up.

Task 47

Time allowed:
Reading/marking changes 5 mins
Typing 15 mins
Checking/correcting 5 mins
25 mins

P R A X I   G R O U P   L I M I T E D

Re-siting Committee

Meeting to be held on Tuesday 5 January 1988 at 1400 hrs in the Board Room, Head Office

A G E N D A

1. Apologies for absence
2. Minutes of last meeting held 14 July 1989 (circulated)
3. Matters Arising
   3.1 The Hampstead site has been purchased & the Group's solicitors advise vacant possession will be taken from 1st March 1990.

4. Re-planning
   4.1 To consider advisability & need for plans regarding the previously projected move to Moreton to be re-structured in view of the purchase at Hampstead.
   4.2 In the light of decisions in 4.1, to consider strategies to ensure maximum benefit is derived from work already done.

5. Accom
   5.1 Cttee members will have noted that fewer rooms will be available for staff at Hampstead than had been envisaged at Moreton. More shared offices will need to be by staff. (To receive report from Mrs Anders)
   5.2 To consider whether representation from staff association & unions should be sought on this Cttee.

6. Appointments
   6.1 To consider the appointment of extra members to this Cttee.
   (Note: decisions taken under Item 5 could affect Cttee's deliberations here)
   6.2 Selection of a Cttee member to attend Senior Management Cttee meetings - see memo attached, doc 11/ATS/90.
7. Any other business.
8. Date of next meeting.

Change Hamsted to Hampstead every time

f) Alternative spellings

If a draft contains the word 'organise', for example, and you usually spell it as 'organize' you need not change your habit in the exam. This applies **only** to words for which alternative spellings can be found in an English dictionary.

No words of this type will be deliberately spelt both ways in order to test your spelling. Therefore, you may copy what is written in the exam paper, **or** you may use your normal spelling if that is different. Be careful not to mix the two if the word occurs more than once in a task.

g) Fractions

Always type fractions that are not included on your keyboard in the same style.

For example, if three fractions occur in an exam task and only one of them is included on the keyboard of your machine, you should of course type the one available on your machine, and make up the other two **either** in 'sloping' style, e.g.

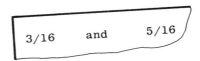

or by use of superscript (superior) and subscript (inferior) characters, e.g.

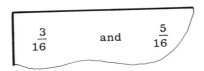

- ■ USE THE FRACTIONS ON YOUR MACHINE whenever they are required in the exam.

- ■ TYPE OTHERS in a CONSISTENT STYLE.

h) Line spacing

When there is no instruction in the draft to use a particular line spacing you must **decide** what line spacing to use, taking account of:

- amount of material;
- type and size of stationery available;
- purpose of the document to be typed.

No penalty will be incurred if you deliberately change your line spacing to emphasise a particular section of a document, e.g. a quotation or extract that will be highlighted by a change of line spacing.

Identical items

You will be asked to look for and change only items that are exactly the same, e.g.

'Change "Denis" to "Dennis" each time.'
'Change the word "Teeline" to "shorthand" throughout.'

Make notes

This type of instruction requires you to practise skills similar to those used in proof-reading. It is not difficult, but demands concentration. Work-based material is often repetitive and not of immediate interest to the typist, but if you let your attention wander while typing, it is easy to miss items that should be changed. The easiest and most reliable method is to read and amend the draft before you start to type.

- SPOTTING items to be changed or corrected is part of proof-reading.

- READ CAREFULLY – you cannot expect everything to be interesting.

- A written note is more reliable than trying to remember.

- DON'T let a simple job cause you unnecessary penalties.

PRACTICE MATERIAL

Practise applying an instruction, once given, throughout the following tasks:

Task 46

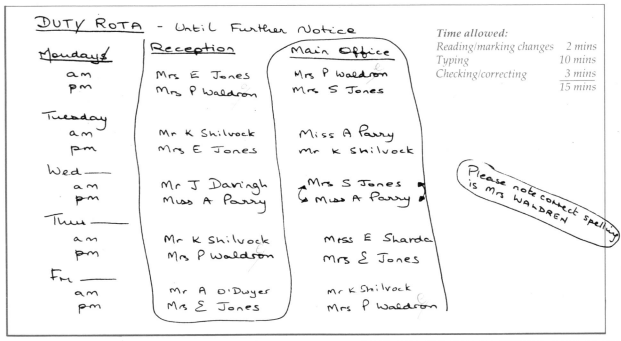

You will incur a presentation fault only if, without good reason, you change line spacing in the same type of item, or section, within a task. (See also syllabus items C6 and C7 on pages 65 and 66.)

> ■ The syllabus allows you to use your own preferred styles. It is necessary to use ONLY ONE STYLE THROUGHOUT A TASK for the items which are listed C3 (a)–(h) on page 6.

C4   GIVING EMPHASIS

Implied instructions

In Part 1 of the exam the draft may include items (such as headings) written in capitals or spaced capitals. Some words will be emphasised by initial capitals and underlining.

You should copy the writer's implied instructions to emphasise words, e.g.

To be typed as:

P R A X I   P R I N C E

The highly popular CARAVAN for holiday touring.

The highly popular CARAVAN for holiday touring.

The Prince is highly versatile.

The Prince is highly versatile.

INSETTING
Short passages may be highlighted by being inset:

To be typed as:

It is most important, therefore, that:

NO MEMBER OF STAFF uses
STAIRCASE A between
10 and 11 am tomorrow.

Please ensure all staff are informed.

It is most important, therefore, that:

NO MEMBER OF STAFF uses
STAIRCASE A between
10 and 11 am tomorrow.

Please ensure all staff are informed.

Throughout both parts of the exam, all words must be typed accurately and in the right order after you have incorporated amendments and instructions given in the draft.

In Part 2, however, you will **not** be required to:

a) **supply** document dates (although you may have to copy dates as shown);

b) **locate** information;

c) **provide spellings** for abbreviated words;

d) **insert** special marks;

e) **indicate** enclosures;

f) **address** labels;

g) **correct** material containing errors (you must, of course, correct any errors you make yourself);

h) **route** carbon copies.

Part 2 tasks **will** include:

a) amendments to text (see B3 on page 34)

b) words that may be of foreign origin or unfamiliar to you (see B8 on page 47).

- ALL WORDS must be ACCURATE.

- RIGHT WORDS in the WRONG ORDER incur Accuracy fault penalties.

- COPY ACCURATELY. Take special care with unfamiliar words, e.g. product names.

B11   INSTRUCTIONS GIVEN ONCE IN A TASK

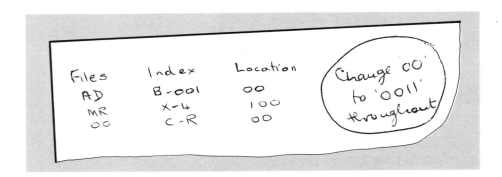

This type of instruction may appear in any task in Part 2 of the exam. The item to be amended (in this case '00') will appear three to five times within the task and you must make the amendment (e.g. change it to '0011') every time without having to be reminded.

No instructions will be given about the exact number of spaces to inset material. You should **decide** how to fulfil the general requirement shown in the draft, taking account of the following:

- Insetting is used to emphasise items so that they stand out and can be quickly and easily seen.
- Narrow insets (e.g. only three spaces) will not achieve the above aim if you are using very wide typing lines.
- A narrow inset may be sufficient to make the insetting 'stand out' from a short typing line, e.g. on A5 paper with the shorter edge at the top.
- It is never wrong to follow the draft in such cases. For example, if the writer has apparently used an inset of about 25 mm (1 in.) at each side, you may do the same; or if an inset of about 38 mm (1½ ins.) is shown at the left side only, you may present your work in this style.

Explicit instructions

Exam drafts may also include written instructions to change items, that is, to use capitals/spaced capitals, initial capitals and/or underlining, or to inset:

Implications - Capitals

Inaccurate data can have very serious consequences.

Checking (use spaced caps)

The procedure must be followed carefully by all.

In particular:

Item 4 - Planning
Example 8 - paragraph design.

Inset

To be typed as:

IMPLICATIONS

<u>Inaccurate data</u> can have very serious consequences.

C H E C K I N G

The procedure must be followed carefully by <u>all</u>. In particular:

        Item 4 - Planning
        Example 8 - paragraph design.

IMPROVING YOUR RATE OF PRODUCTION

1 **re-arranging material**

   a) Develop your own method (an example is given on page 94).

   b) Practise your method until you have a quick and accurate routine.

   c) Practise your routine in different categories, e.g. rearrange your work in: alphabetical order; order of size; numerical sequence; date order (chronologically).

2 **modifying layout**

   a) Have patience to interpret instructions accurately.

   b) Draft yourself an outline of new layout(s).

   c) Always
      i)   check measurements, and count items;
      ii) double-check instructions before typing;
      iii) keep an eye on your time. Getting it right first time is important and quicker in the end.

3 **choosing stationery**

   If in doubt use a **count/check/recall/check** routine (see pages 79–80).

4 **completing forms**

   a) Practise using the interliner for short items; e.g. making deletions and typing in boxes.

   b) Practise using variable line-spacing mechanism to align the typing line over pre-printed lines.

   c) Set tabs for typing series of items between pre-printed vertical lines.

5 **ruling**

   a) Remember to leave space for ruling round material in columns.

   b) Always have the draft close at hand to make sure you copy all of the ruling as required.

   c) Check that paper is straight **and** ruler is straight to avoid sloping lines.

   d) Practise ruling at approximately equal distance from surrounding typed items (don't risk ruling through typing).

   e) Get used to your pen so that you can rule fluently with neat joins and without smudges!

PRACTICE MATERIAL

Practice material is likely to be more difficult than the exam, to ensure you are well-prepared. Tasks may also continue to provide practice on items in Part 1 – which of course will not happen in the exam.

Type the following tasks:

Task 43

Memo

From: A J BENFORD
To   DEALER STORES - B Ball

Take 2 carbon copies - 1 for N Singh 'for information'

Time allowed:
Preparation   3 mins
Typing   5 mins
Checking/correcting   3 mins
                 11 mins

M A S O N   B U I L D

The above firm are NOT to be supplied with counter sales unless CASH is paid at time of collection.

This instruction applies to all items and is to be implemented with effect from TODAY.

In the case of any query contact me or John Naylor on Ext 421. In our absence Najrit Singh will advise, on Ext 429.

Task 44

Time allowed:
Preparation   3 mins
Typing   10 mins
Checking/correcting   5 mins
                 18 mins

T H E   P R I V A T E   S E C T O R

Type heading in ordinary, closed capitals

You wl have noticed that in the title of this talk I refer to the development of management as an art in the private Sector. // I have a strong disinclination to talk on subjects outside my own personal exp. I bel it is in the Private S—— that much of the development of management + of management concepts is taking place at the present time.

Within my Co, as long as we reward the shareholders, we can change - within reason - in any way we wish. We have great freedom in what we make & how we make it, + where we make it.

CAPS
Choosing to work
                 totally
People are no longer dependent upon a job for the basic necessities of life. They CAN and DO choose. But we must have a degree of commitment, skill + enthusiasm for our task, albeit generated + expressed in ways so def different from in the past.

When you have typed this Task check you have used all of the methods of giving emphasis as shown in the draft above.

Section Four

The Part 2 Exam

11   *Rate of Production*

In Part 2 of the exam you are expected to:

1 complete a printed form with information given to you;
2 type a notice or a draft advertisement;
3 type and rule a table

You must finish all three tasks, subject to the fact that a few words (not exceeding seven) may be counted as omissions and penalised as Accuracy faults.

GENERAL INSTRUCTIONS IN PART 2

Part 2 tests your ability to carry out modifications from general instructions, that is, without the use of arrows and other signs showing where each and every item must be typed within, say, a list required in alphabetical order.

This is different from the work in Part 1, which tests your ability to work fluently from drafts in which the required changes have been made in handwriting, or if words and figures are to be moved, their new positions are clearly shown by balloons, arrows, insertion marks, etc.

FEWER WORDS IN PART 2

You will need more time to plan your work, so there are fewer words to be typed in Part 2 than in Part 1.
It is easy to overrun, if you take too much time for analysing tasks to see what is required and for drafting your outline of new shapes or where material is to be placed.

C6 SPECIFIED LINE SPACING

One task in Part 1 will include an instruction to use a particular line spacing for a section of the document.

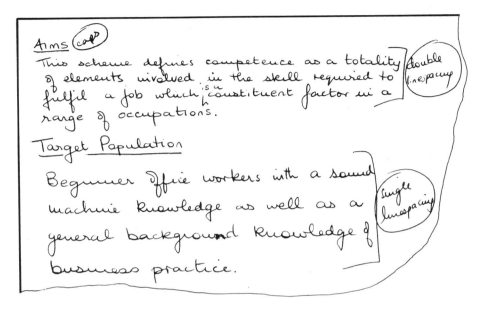

To be typed as:

AIMS

This scheme defines competence as a totality of elements

involved in the skill required to fulfil a job which is

a constituent factor in a range of occupations.

Target Population

Beginner office workers with a sound machine knowledge
as well as a general background knowledge of business
practice.

Providing you know how to use the line-space regulator of your machine there is nothing difficult about following these instructions, but **care** is always needed to make sure that a simple requirement, well within your capabilities, does not cause you unnecessary penalties in the exam.

- SINGLE-LINE SPACING means no clear line space between lines of type in the text.

- DOUBLE-LINE SPACING means one clear line space after each line of type in the text.

- DON'T miss, forget or ignore instructions.

- DON'T forget to return to original line spacing for the rest of the task after the instruction has been carried out.

In the exam, presentation faults will be counted for entries which are more than one line space above or below their proper place. Of course, word faults will be counted if the wrong information is entered (or if errors occur within the correct word(s)).

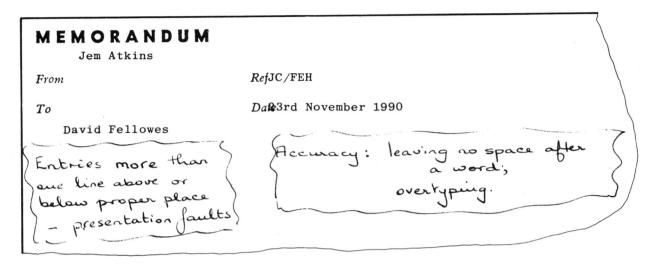

MEMORANDUM

Jem Atkins

From

To

David Fellowes

Entries more than one line above or below proper place — presentation faults

RefJC/FEH

Date 3rd November 1990

Accuracy: leaving no space after a word; overtyping.

Spaces after pre-printed headings

There must be **at least one** space after every word, including those printed on forms.

Some typists prefer to leave the same number of spaces after each heading; others prefer to vary the number of spaces so as to type entries immediately below each other:

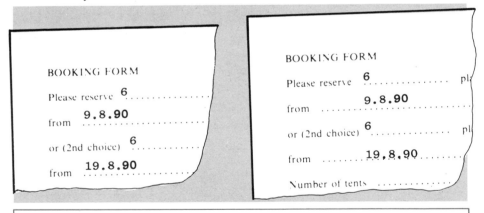

- DON'T OVERTYPE pre-printing.
- AT LEAST ONE SPACE must be left AFTER pre-printed items.
- COPY REFERENCES EXACTLY (they may be computer codes in which precision is important).
- DO NOT ADD references if they are not given (you cannot assume your style of referencing is used in **all** offices and is appropriate for **any** task).

TIMED EXAM PRACTICE FOR PART 1

Type the three Part 1 tasks in each of the past Stage II exam papers in Section Five. Then complete the personal progress record – in the stationery section at the back of the book – to monitor your progress.

RSA Typewriting Skills Book Two   Part 1: Presentation

Practice changing line spacing and insetting. Remember to change back to original line spacing and margins.

Task 45

(Type on plain A5)

The following advert recently appeared in the Yorkshire Gazette:

(single-line spacing)

"A variety of goods available as suitable for yr car boot sale. Contact us for goods to supplement and enliven yr stock."

Are some firms now acting as wholesalers for the car boot "retailer"?

Should some goods at these sales be marked "Specially bought-in for the sale"?

Inspectors shd visit Sunday markets with this in mind. Please research appropriate bye-laws.

C7   ALLOCATING SPACE

(Leave 4 clear line spaces at ·X·)

People in this job will be assessed by
·X·
A range of objectives set by their supervisors & themselves for the year
·X·
Checklist items agreed for their Job Specification
·X·
Practical performance

In Part 1 of the exam you will be instructed to leave a given number of line spaces in one of the tasks. The instructions may refer to up to three places within the same document, as in the example above.

Be precise

There is no requirement to do other than what is requested in the draft, that is, to leave the exact number of line spaces clear at the point(s) indicated.

Count

To carry out the instruction, 'Leave 7 clear lines':

- type the last line of text above the point where the space is to be left;
- make sure your machine is set up for single-line spacing;
- turn up the number of lines instructed (seven in this example);
- turn up once more in order to leave the seventh line clear.

> ■ The EXACT number of lines requested must be left clear.
>
> ■ SET YOUR MACHINE TO SINGLE-LINE SPACING FOR COUNTING.
>
> ■ DON'T type on the last line in your clear space.

C11   TYPING ON LETTERHEADS AND MEMO FORMS

MEMORANDUM

From Bench Section

To Assembly/Mr Martinson

Ref Dianne

Date 19 March 1990

PRAXITELES GROUP

A fictitious organisation for examination purposes only

PRAXITELES HOUSE · ADAM STREET · LONDON WC2N 6EZ

TELEPHONE 01 930 5115

Our ref XD-4/1

Your ref ExpSales/HE

19 January 1990

United Oceanways Shipping Co
Atlantic House
Dredgington Dock
SOUTHAMPTON   SO41 16BX

Alignment

You will want to present your work as attractively as possible, and one of the ways in which you can improve its appearance is to make sure that entries typed after pre-printed headings result in a line as level as possible.

RSA
STATIONERY PAD

In order to help you prepare for the RSA Typewriting Skills Stage II exam, twenty-seven of the tasks in this book require the use of special RSA stationery, the same design as used in the exam. On the next twenty-four pages, you will find all the blank stationery that you need to complete these tasks. The stationery includes six Praxiteles Group letterheads (this is the RSA's fictional organisation for exam purposes), seven memos and nine forms to be filled in with information given in the relevant tasks. In the examinations the stationery provided is A4/A5 size. In this book the stationery is slightly smaller than A4/A5 and users of the book should take account of this – especially in relation to letterheads and memos.

The stationery is the copyright of the RSA Examinations Board and must not be photocopied, with the sole exception of the 2 forms which accompany the 1989 examination papers. Stationery pads containing ten replacement sets of stationery (that is, enough for ten students) can be purchased direct from Heinemann Educational Books Ltd, Freepost NH3746, Sanders Lodge Industrial Estate, Rushden, Northamptonshire NN10 9BR. Please write in with your order (no stamp required).

ISBN 0 435 45181 2   240 pp per pad (enough for ten students) 297 x 210 mm

PERSONAL PROGRESS RECORD: TIMED EXAM PRACTICE

	Time taken	No. of word faults	No. of presentation faults	Likely result*
PART 1 OF THE EXAM **Tasks 34 – 36** Continuous text (Task 34) Memo (Task 35) Letter (Task 36)				
TOTAL:				
Pilot scheme, Summer 1990 Letter (Task 1) Memo (Task 2) Continuous text (Task 3)				
TOTAL:				
Specimen paper, Summer 1990 Letter (Task 1) Continuous text (Task 2) Memo (Task 3)				
TOTAL:				
PART 2 OF THE EXAM **Pilot Scheme, Summer 1990** Advert (Task 4) Ruled table (Task 5) Form (Task 6)				
TOTAL:				
Specimen paper, Summer 1990 Form (Task 4) Advert (Task 5) Ruled table (Task 6)				
TOTAL:				

★ To be awarded a **Pass in Part 1** of the exam you must complete all three tasks (in 1 1/4 hours) with no more than **eleven** Accuracy faults and **eight** Presentation faults. To be awarded a **Pass in Part 2** you must complete all three tasks with no more than **seven** Accuracy faults and **five** Presentation faults.

To be eligible for **Distinction in Part 1** you must finish all three tasks (in 1 1/4 hours) with no more than **four** Accuracy faults and **four** Presentation faults. To achieve **Distinction in Part 2** you must complete the three tasks with no more than **three** Accuracy faults and **three** Presentation faults.

PRAXITELES GROUP

A fictitious organisation for examination purposes only

PRAXITELES HOUSE · ADAM STREET · LONDON WC2N 6EZ
TELEPHONE 01 930 5115

Our ref

Your ref

EXAMINATIONS BOARD

TYPEWRITING SKILLS STAGE II – Summer Series 1989 – 288

Centre Number	YOUR NAMES

THIS FORM—FOR USE IN WORKING TASK 6—MUST BE INSERTED INSIDE THE COVER OF YOUR ANSWER BOOK AT THE CONCLUSION OF THE EXAMINATION. IF BOTH SIDES OF THIS FORM ARE USED ONE ATTEMPT MUST BE CANCELLED.

ORDER FORM

CUSTOMER'S NAME AND ADDRESS	TELEPHONE NO Daytime No only	
	DATE	
	AGENT'S REFERENCE	OPC 666
TOUR NO:	NO OF CLIENTS	

MR/MRS MISS/MSTR	INIT	SURNAME	ROOM TYPE	TOUR PRICE	SUPPLEMENTS ie private facilities etc	
				£		£
				£		£
				£		£
				£		£
				£		£

Balcony   YES/NO*

*Delete as necessary

SUB TOTAL	£	TOTAL £
SUPPLEMENTS	£	
TOTAL TOUR PRICE	£	

DEPOSIT PAID	£
INSURANCE PAID	£
TOTAL PAID	£
BALANCE	£

If you wish to pay by Barclaycard
or Access please tick the appropriate box

VISA ☐   ACCESS ☐

☐☐☐☐☐☐☐☐☐☐☐☐☐☐☐☐☐☐

PRAXITELES GROUP

A fictitious organisation for examination purposes only

PRAXITELES HOUSE · ADAM STREET · LONDON WC2N 6EZ
TELEPHONE 01 930 5115

Our ref

Your ref

EXAMINATIONS BOARD

TYPEWRITING SKILLS STAGE II — Whitsun Series 1989 – 288

Centre Number	YOUR NAMES

THIS FORM—FOR USE IN WORKING TASK 6—MUST BE INSERTED INSIDE THE COVER OF YOUR ANSWER BOOK AT THE CONCLUSION OF THE EXAMINATION. IF BOTH SIDES OF THIS FORM ARE USED ONE ATTEMPT MUST BE CANCELLED.

EXPENDITURE APPLICATION

Name: Ref No:

Address: Date:

		Unit Price	Total Price
		£	£
Function: Brief Details: Date: Catering: No. attending: Additional requirements:			
Copy correspondence * delete as appropriate	Enclosed/not enclosed*		
		Total	£

PRAXITELES GROUP

A fictitious organisation for examination purposes only

PRAXITELES HOUSE · ADAM STREET · LONDON WC2N 6EZ
TELEPHONE 01 930 5115

Our ref

Your ref

PRAXITELES GROUP

PRAXITELES HOUSE · ADAM STREET · LONDON WC2N 6EZ
TELEPHONE 01 930 5115

Our ref

Your ref

ENQUIRY

To:

Dear Sirs

Please let us have, as soon as possible, your best price, terms and conditions for the following:

Details

Please mark your reply for the attention of ....

....

Yours faithfully
PRAXITELES GROUP

Contracts/Purchasing Department*

*Delete as appropriate

PRAXITELES GROUP

PRAXITELES HOUSE · ADAM STREET · LONDON WC2N 6EZ
TELEPHONE 01 930 5115

Our ref

Your ref

JOB LIST

*Department/Sector/Division:

No.	Job	Required by:
1		
2		
3		
4		
5		
6		

*Delete as appropriate

PRAXITELES GROUP

PRAXITELES HOUSE · ADAM STREET · LONDON WC2N 6EZ
TELEPHONE 01 930 5115

Our ref

Your ref

Sector: Period:................. to............................ Issued to: Staff/Supervisor/Operatives*		**Action List**
Contract ref.	Job details	Person responsible
	Date issued	

*Delete as appropriate

PRAXITELES GROUP

PRAXITELES HOUSE · ADAM STREET · LONDON WC2N 6EZ
TELEPHONE 01 930 5115

Our ref

Your ref

PRAXITELES GROUP

PRAXITELES HOUSE · ADAM STREET · LONDON WC2N 6EZ
TELEPHONE 01 930 5115

REMITTANCE ADVICE

To ....

....

....

Date ....

Cheque enclosed/Credit made to your bank*
in settlement of the following:

Date	Invoice No.	Amount £
	Total	£

*Delete as appropriate

MEMORANDUM

From   *Ref*

To   *Date*

ORDER

PRAXITELES GROUP

PRAXITELES HOUSE · ADAM STREET
LONDON WC2N 6EZ
TELEPHONE 01 930 5115

To: ....

....

....

....

....

No:	Date:

Please supply:

Deliver to: *Above address/Following address

Required by:	Signed:
	Department:

*Delete as appropriate

MEMORANDUM

From   *Ref*

To   *Date*

ORDER

To: ....

....

....

....

....

PRAXITELES GROUP

PRAXITELES HOUSE · ADAM STREET
LONDON WC2N 6EZ

TELEPHONE 01 930 5115

No:	Date:

Please supply:

Deliver to: *Above address/Following address

Required by:	Signed:
	Department:

*Delete as appropriate

MEMORANDUM

From

To

Ref

Date

PRAXITELES GROUP

A fictitious organisation for examination purposes only

PRAXITELES HOUSE · ADAM STREET · LONDON WC2N 6EZ
TELEPHONE 01 930 5115

Our ref

Your ref

QUOTATION

Dear Sirs

We are pleased to quote as follows:

Item	Ref. No.	Price	Delivery date

Terms ....   Carriage ....

We look forward to receipt of your order.

Yours faithfully

*Sales Enquiries Department / Special Contracts Division

*Delete as appropriate

MEMORANDUM

From   *Ref*

To   *Date*

PRAXITELES GROUP

A fictitious organisation for examination purposes only

PRAXITELES HOUSE · ADAM STREET · LONDON WC2N 6EZ
TELEPHONE 01 930 5115

Our ref

Your ref

QUOTATION

Dear Sirs

We are pleased to quote as follows:

Item	Ref. No.	Price	Delivery date

Terms .... 　　　　　Carriage ....

We look forward to receipt of your order.

Yours faithfully

*Sales Enquiries Department / Special Contracts Division

*Delete as appropriate

MEMORANDUM

From *Ref*

To *Date*

MEMORANDUM

From   *Ref*

To   *Date*